THE
RING
OF THE
WAY

Other books by Taisen Deshimaru
published in English

I SHIN DEN SHIN

THE RING OF THE WAY

Testament of a Zen Master

TAISEN DESHIMARU

Compiled by Evelyn de Smedt and Dominique Dussaussoy
Translated by Nancy Amphoux

E. P. DUTTON   NEW YORK

Published in the United States by E. P. Dutton,
a division of NAL Penguin Inc.,
2 Park Avenue, New York, N.Y. 10016.

Published simultaneously in Canada by
Fitzhenry and Whiteside Limited, Toronto.

Originally published in France under the title *L'anneau de la Voie*.

Library of Congress Cataloging-in-Publication Data

Deshimaru, Taisen.
The ring of the way.
Translation of: L'anneau de la voie.
1. Sōtōshū—Doctrines. 2. Spiritual life (Zen
Buddhism) I. Smedt, Evelyn de. II. Dussaussoy, Dominique.
III. Title.
BQ9418.7.D4713   1987   294.3'927   86-29193
ISBN: 0-525-48293-8

W

Designed by Earl Tidwell
The calligraphy in this book is by Jacques Foussadier-Kugen.

1 3 5 7 9 10 8 6 4 2
First American Edition

CONTENTS

ESSENCE AND PHENOMENA INTERMINGLE

TRANSLATOR'S
PREFACE

———

You can take this book a sentence at a time. It may not be easy to take it any other way! Some of the sentences are short and tough and imply that most of us, however much we think we have control of the universe and our private lives, are firmly grasping the wrong end of the stick. Some of them are long and full of abstract philosophical terms and are none too clear, even if you do know what the abstract words mean. Some of them sound very highfalutin, a little like high priests in Tolkien, and some sound like poetry that's over before it starts.

Why?

When Taisen Deshimaru Roshi died, one or two of his disciples, feeling helpless and yet impelled to get busy at once, decided to sort through his fifteen published volumes of teaching and commentary on the teachings of his predecessors, plus a stack several feet high of magazine articles, lectures, talks, manuscript notes, and typescripts of things he'd said here, there, and everywhere, and produce one slim volume containing the gist of it all.

This is it, and of course it has all the things wrong with it that one could imagine as the result of such a procedure.

For instance, it contains almost verbatim quotes of passages from fifteen or twenty ancient texts, Chinese and Japanese, stuck next to each other sometimes without any commentary between; and there is no way to tell which bit is from Dogen in the thirteenth century and which bit is from something Sekito wrote in the ninth and which is pure Deshimaru in the twentieth.

But it doesn't matter. This testament to the activity of an enormous personality is in the purest tradition of the East, where wisdom is not protected by copyright, and learning to be a master involves primarily learning at great length and in exhaustive detail, and copying, what all the other masters since the beginning of time have said and done, played, written, painted, and so on. (Not that anybody ever sets out to "learn to be a master.")

It is also extremely repetitive, although some of the repetitions have been eliminated out of consideration for readers who do not practice zazen (because those who do practice zazen know that nothing is ever the same twice, even if they have already heard it in the very same words six times this morning). The repetitions also have something to do with the way people think in the East, or rather the way they approach material they want to think or talk about; but most importantly, they are not, I repeat, repetitions.

People have said that Deshimaru was highly traditional, meaning that he seemed to insist on using a lot of Japanese words and urged his disciples to wear black robes and chant in the original language; this was meant as a criticism. People have also said that he was unorthodox, meaning that he gallivanted around the world and went to live in Paris instead of sticking to some temple in Japan, that he did not at all mind appearing on television to demonstrate zazen, and that he very much wanted to meet and talk with prominent scientists, for instance, to exchange and compare notes with them; most of the time this was intended as a criticism, too.

He was a master, which means he was both traditional and unorthodox, and not only in the superficial matters reflected in the criticism. That is exactly what a master is. That is probably what we should all be: coming loyally out of our past, honestly assuming all of it without cults or cover-ups, and freely creating our present. Deshimaru Roshi did it and tried to teach others how to do it; and a tiny little bit of the "how" is contained in this jumbled, roaring, windswept silence of a book.

COMPILERS' PREFACE

Go back to the source, the place where it all begins. Learn what we really are and mean, find the true self.

This is and has always been the core of every religion and philosophy; it is the clear stream that wells up from the regular practice of zazen.

Buddha-nature: total, universal, divine nature; the purest condition that can be, the natural and original condition of our consciousness. The closer we come to that state of consciousness, pure spirit, pure mind, the more we radiate light. The further we move from it, the more easily we are eaten up by our environment.

If we open our hands, we can receive anything; if we are empty, we can contain the whole universe. Empty is the mind that attaches itself to nothing and lives the present moment, lives that and nothing else.

The one basic practice, the experience of the source, is zazen. It transcends space and time. Shakyamuni Buddha rediscovered it twenty-five centuries ago: the immemorial posture transmitted directly from master to disciple, age to age, continent to continent. From India to China with Bodhidharma in the sixth century; from China to Japan with Dogen in the thirteenth; from Japan to Europe with Taisen Deshimaru in the twentieth, the seated posture has always been the ultimate "secret" of Buddhism.

Heir to the long lineage of the masters of transmission, Taisen Deshimaru came to Europe twenty years ago to transmit true Zen. A spiritual friend and respected master, he devoted all his strength and all his energy to educating his many disciples, making it possible for them to have the experience of not-two, non-duality, to touch the divine nature present in each of them and see the path that leads to the apprehension of nothingness.

> *All existences are like the leaves on the tree:*
> *Fed by the one root.*
> *Origin and end come from the same source, empty;*
> *Origin and end alike go back to that.*

Taisen Deshimaru died on April 30, 1982, leaving to his disciples the essence of his teaching and the mission of transmitting the practice of zazen to others.

The ring of the way has no beginning and no end.

It is repeating the experience that is taking place here and now, and it bears eternity within it.

The words of a Zen master, of many Zen masters of the past intermingled, transmitted from patriarch to patriarch beyond time and phenomena, beyond thinking and not-thinking: this book is the trace left by the oral teaching of the masters since Shakyamuni Buddha.

Eyes horizontal,
Nose vertical:
Essence of Buddhism

ZEN
IS
ZAZEN

———

When somebody asks you
What is True Buddhism,
You don't need to open your mouth
To explain.
Please: Just show them all the faces
Of your zazen posture.
Then the spring breeze will blow,
Tease open the dazzling blossom of the early plum.

Zen is just sitting; Zen is just exactly zazen.

For many people, Zen is yet another Oriental religion, but although it grew up within the most ancient of Buddhist traditions, it is like a spring that wells up endlessly fresh. It is always modern, always alive, making itself over again every instant. Zen is not reasoning or theory or ideas. Not knowledge to grasp with the mind. It is only a practice, and that practice is zazen, right meditation, right sitting.

Re-creating oneself, understanding one's real self, and not austerity or mortification: the gateway to peace and freedom.

The only real, worthwhile revolution is turned inward; it is the revolution of our mind and it results from the practice of Zen, a profound philosophy that cannot be grasped by rational thought alone.

What is the practice of Zen, what is zazen? *Zen* means "concentration of the mind," and *za* means "seated." The term comes to us in its present form, *zazen,* from Japanese. Before that, *zen* was *ch'an,* in Chinese, and before that again it was *dyana,* in Sanskrit.

FUKANZAZENGI

THE WHAT AND HOW OF ZAZEN
ACCORDING TO MASTER DOGEN

Forget about any kind of practice or ritual that is founded on intellectual knowledge, that runs after words and follows only the letter of things. Instead, learn to make the half-turn that throws your light within and shows you your true nature. Body and mind will drop away of themselves, and your real face will appear.

If you want to get to that-which-is, then practice that-which-is right away.

For zazen, a quiet room is best. Eat and drink moderately. Do not think, "This thing is good, that one bad." Do not be for or against. Stop all movements of the conscious mind. Do not form judgments about thoughts or perceptions. Do not want to become a Buddha. Zazen has absolutely nothing to do with positions of sitting or lying down.

In the place where you ordinarily sit, place a thick mat and a firm cushion on top of it. Sit down in the full or half-lotus position. In the full lotus you first place your right foot on your left thigh and then your left foot on your right thigh. In the half-lotus you simply press the left foot against the right thigh.

Make sure that your clothing doesn't bind you, loosen your belt, arrange your garments neatly.

Now place your right hand on your left leg, palm up, and your left hand, also palm up, in your right hand so that the tips of your thumbs just touch.

Sit up very straight in the correct attitude, leaning neither left nor right, neither forward nor backward.

See that your ears are just above your shoulders and your nose on a line with your navel.

Place your tongue against the front of the palate, mouth closed, teeth just touching.

Your eyes must always be open, and you must breathe gently through your nose.

When you have placed yourself in the right posture, breathe deeply once, in and out. Sway right and left several times, then come to a stop and sit, firm and resolute.

Zen is beyond dualism. It is utter simplicity, but it opens the door to absolute wisdom. That door, the full meaning of zazen, is *shikantaza*, only sit; sit and do no other thing at all.

If there is a doctrine in Zen, it is "What for? For nothing," for no particular reason, no goal or advantage. Everyone is always working for some goal, idea, or objective, everyone wants to give and receive; but the highest spiritual life is achieved only where there is no trying to gain anything and no fear of losing anything.

Keep your hands open, and all the sands of the desert can pass through them. Close them, and all you can feel is a bit of grit.

The tiniest notion in the conscious mind of holding back, of hanging on, is an obstacle. To be in harmony with the cosmic system means letting go of everything. Then we become unity, and can take in fresh energy from the cosmos.

———

Our educational systems are based too much on intellectual attainments; our traditional religions and codes of behavior no longer seem able to provide solutions. We are full of anxiety, unsure, we don't know which course to follow, we cannot keep our balance, and so we escape into whatever gives instant gratification, whatever is easy. Every time we do that, we move further away from the spiritual essence and real meaning of humanity. Contradictions abound, dissatisfaction is rife, the natural human balance has been destroyed because the very idea of living in a normal condition of body and mind has lost all meaning for most of us.

Studying the Way of the Buddha means studying the self.
Studying the self means forgetting the self.
Forgetting the self means being confirmed by every existence in the cosmos.
Being confirmed by every existence in the cosmos means that both body and mind have dropped away; and when one's own body and mind have dropped away, then so have those of every other person and thing.

What is the nucleus, the essence of every religion and philosophy? Understanding oneself. Know thyself. Not just with the imagination or the logical, reasoning, front part of the brain, but with the whole body.

Cosmic energy is what makes us live. During zazen our consciousness and body harmonize with the cosmic system, by means of our breathing. Our five senses and our consciousness become calm and shed all worries and fears, naturally, automatically, unconsciously. That is true religion.

The very particular posture of zazen influences consciousness, sensations, thoughts. Zazen is the return to the normal condition, the natural health of the body. If the body is sick, zazen will be more difficult. Zazen is a barometer of the health of body and mind.

Sickness and disease arise as a result of distortions and imbalances in the body and mind. Through the zazen posture you can

5

identify all the places in you that are twisted or weak. Zazen means looking at yourself, understanding your own ego, your karma, all the bad habits of your body and mind.

When you practice zazen, you are in a completely balanced posture for many minutes at a time. Desires and thoughts drift up from your unconscious, and you can observe yourself. If you feel a pain in some part of your body, or a difference between left and right sides, that could be a sign of something wrong now or in the future.

Almost every religion tries to establish control over the mind; but if you try to control mind by mind, you become complicated. Using the personal will to gain control of the mind is, in the end, like drinking to cure a hangover.

Zen education is not scientific. Zen education is beyond science, beyond philosophy. Zen thinking is practiced through the body. It embraces all contradictions.

In Zen, the existence or nonexistence of a substance is not a problem to be thought about. In Zen, the problems we set ourselves are these: What must I do? How must I be here and now?

Kodo Sawaki (my master) used to say that living our lives is like riding a bicycle. You have to have practice. If body and brain are too stiff, you cannot do it, you cannot keep your balance. To ride a bicycle you have to pedal all the time. If you don't pedal you don't go forward, and if you lean over too far you fall down.

We have to use our brain like a bicycle. In this exact instant, act in that exact way. Each instant is different. Here-and-now changes every instant, so our brains must not be one-sided. If we decide things according to our own mental categories alone, our brain does not develop and we cannot act with wisdom.

From the question "How am I?" we must move on to the question "How should I be, in my life?" At that point, the high truth of the practice of faith and religion can assume many dimensions. What is of prime importance is to begin to practice, to experience.

6

In Zen, even judgments about good and evil must be abandoned. Good and evil are two sides of the same coin. If we are attached to a judgment, it becomes fixed and acquires a substance of its own. That is why in Zen there is nothing but negating, forever saying no to every statement. But what is left at the end of the statements is not negative.

> *The middle way*
> *Is control,*
> *Balance.*

Recently, religions have been spending too much time on teaching, sutras and chants, study, doctrine, theology. Practice has been forgotten, and faith. But without practice and faith, people cannot wake up.

Wind and waves are always moving across our minds. Human beings create their own illusions. Running after the shadows in our consciousness leads to illusions and mistakes. Most people speak out of their own limited, mistaken illusions. What they say is wrong because they make value decisions on the basis of their illusions. Illusions are caused by the shifting mind, which moves and strays in response to its environment; whereas satori is the original, normal, stable condition of the mind. The contents of our conceptions and categories shift from moment to moment. Nothing in them is fixed, unmoving.

In the visible world nothing is identical to anything else; every object is different.

Everything exists by virtue of interdependence and has no permanence, no lasting substance.

During zazen, the brain is like a window through which a fresh breeze blows.

> *Spotless, the moonlight reflected*
> *In the waters of the mind.*
> *Even the waves break against it*
> *And shatter into light.*

During zazen, brain and consciousness become pure. It's exactly like muddy water left to stand in a glass. Little by little, the sediment sinks to the bottom and the water becomes pure.

> *People are not aware*
> *Of any precious gem,*
> *But everyone possesses it*
> *Embedded deep in the Alaya consciousness*
> *That is unconscious.*

When the Alaya consciousness emerges and expresses itself, then there is the mirror of wisdom.

In Soto Zen,* satori—an awakening—is a rediscovery of a forgotten original state, beyond anything that can be observed by the reasoning part of the mind. It is not subjective but completely objective.

Zazen, which is the essence of the teaching of the Buddha and patriarchs who came after him, enables us to leave every contradiction behind. It is a leap beyond categories; it is *hishiryo,* unthinking thought, thought that comes out of the heart of unthinking.

Every phenomenon occurring here and now is not distinct from satori; they all go to make up the true satori, the true Buddha-nature. In the nature of Buddha there is neither form nor not-form.

> *Zazen has a simple taste, light, almost neutral.*
> *If you season zazen, you cheapen it.*
> *It is like the broad sky*
> *And the endless ocean.*

Satori is unification, unity, non-separation. Zazen is satori. Actions are proof, confirmation of satori. Satori is not an event; it is a permanent state that continues until death. Even so, you shouldn't wait until you're in your coffin before experiencing it;

*The branch of Chinese Zen Buddhism founded by Dogen in Japan in the thirteenth century; emphasis is on the intensive, wholehearted practice of zazen.

8

it's too late then. For each person, satori is both different and the same, like the moon that is reflected just as completely in a dewdrop, in a drop of dog urine, or on the surface of the ocean.

We have to throw everything away, both body and mind; then zazen accompanies us; we can follow zazen without having to expend our own strength, our own consciousness. Unconsciously, naturally, automatically, we separate from illusions and obtain satori.

Zazen must draw our thoughts toward Buddha, the cosmic order.

The zazen posture is satori. It is like the lion in repose, the dragon's roar. It is deserving of the highest respect.

Seated, standing, or lying down, you should look like the king of lions, always free and strong, brave and fearless forever; if people happen to see your posture, it should radiate so much dignity that they cannot come too close.

All at once, let go of all your thoughts, all the things you know, and if you practice *shikantaza,* sitting in zazen and abandoning everything, little by little you will become acquainted with satori. You will reach the way by using your body properly, especially when sitting in zazen.

People who are looking for understanding based on some limited and selective form of knowledge do not believe in the supreme wisdom of Buddha, which is the product of unlimited cosmic consciousness. If you doubt this supreme wisdom, you will remain a prisoner of your conscious self and suffer eternal dissatisfaction and discomfort. The heart must let itself be carried by faith, must trust naturally and unconsciously to the central brain, instead of clinging to the conscious self. Our minds contain the whole cosmos.

In the world of truth, I and other people are not separate. There, no trace of dualism exists: each one, phenomenon and essence, precedes the other, and the two fit perfectly together.

When the mind does not dwell upon any one thing, true mind appears.

In most forms of meditation and in most religions, Hinduism or Yoga in India, Tibetan Buddhism, Christianity, even some forms of Zen, the practitioners, both masters and disciples, are always trying to destroy their illusions and remain permanently in the state of unthought; to destroy their misled, misleading minds and dwell in the state of no-mind; to kill the living activity within themselves and stagnate in a condition of nonliving nonactivity. Just as they are always trying to destroy characteristics and appearances, and revel in the formless, the undefined. The result of this kind of meditation is that both the religions and the people practicing them have grown weak. True zazen is like a mirror that reflects all forms and all phenomena, in which your mind becomes completely clear.

When your mind grows dark, *kontin**** drops you into the abysses of the demon of sleep, and when it soars, *sanran* hurls you into the caverns of the demon of confusion. So in zazen you must watch out for the two demons of *kontin* and *sanran,* stupor or sleepiness and exaltation. But if you are at the center of the luminous palace of cosmic tranquility, *sanran* fades away of itself and is lost in that perfect tranquility. Then your mind becomes completely quiet, even in the presence of *sanran.* In the same way, the demon of *kontin* can be overcome by observing your own light, and you can become that light wholly, even in the presence of *kontin.*

So during zazen you must observe *kontin* and become luminous with *kontin;* and you must stop *sanran* and become calm with *sanran.* This is like a wild boar that has come upon a gold mine, or the wind spreading afar the scent of sweet-smelling flowers, unconsciously.

In the truly spiritual mind there is no illusion.

If we enjoy perfect freedom of the mind, the white cloud and blue mountain themselves are changed into shadows in our

*Kontin and *sanran,* at the physical level, are used to describe states or conditions of mind during zazen that are not in balance; *kontin* can be simply "falling asleep" and *sanran* "nervous, agitated."

unique thought, and the mist in the pine forest, the snow lying on the bamboo woods, are also changed into shadows in our unique thought. Then we can fish the moonlight and plow the clouds.

At that moment, as the infinitely great merit of zazen is realized, we can put the whole cosmos inside one poppy seed or pour the ocean through one pore of the skin and change the earth of hell into an earth of paradise, unconsciously, naturally, automatically.

Please, my dear disciples, you must consider that our lives are as vain and ephemeral as the dewdrop on the morning grass and that our destiny is as impermanent as a dream or illusion, a bubble or a shadow.

> *When one drop of water falls into the ocean,*
> *When one mote of dust falls upon the earth,*
> *Then the drop of water is no longer a drop of water,*
> *It becomes ocean;*
> *And the mote of dust is no longer a mote of dust,*
> *It becomes the whole earth.*

Real Zen is not running to catch the way, it is being caught by the way. Real Zen is waking up, metamorphosis; it is not a personal satori. The Nirvana Sutra contains these words, spoken by the Buddha when he experienced satori under the bodhi tree: I and all living beings have realized the way together.

Do not practice the Buddha Dharma,* do not practice zazen, for your own benefit or for utilitarian purposes or for honors or for merits or to seek advantages or miracles, but only for the Buddha Dharma. *Shikantaza* is the highest, the greatest, the purest dimension of the human body and mind.

Dogen's Zen is not the desire to become more than human, a special person, a Buddha or God. Nor is it the hope of experiencing emptiness, or of performing miracles. It is a return to the normal condition of the human spirit.

*The teachings, truth, and law of Buddha.

11

The practice of zazen brings inner peace. In addition, your zazen influences all humanity, the entire cosmos.

Zazen is a game, the greatest game of all. Only those who have understood this continue to practice.

SHŪ SHŌ ICHI NYŌ

THE SEVEN
PRINCIPLES OF
DOGEN'S ZEN

If you look for something, you will go wrong.

When you practice zazen you become a saint, Buddha himself.

To educate disciples, to teach, you must concentrate on practice, *shu,* and not wait for satori, *sho.*

1. SHU SHO ICHI NYO

Practice and satori are not two.

Most religions say you must practice, strive, and believe first, and afterwards comes grace, or salvation, or satori. In Dogen's Zen, practice is satori.

2. SHO BUTSU ICHI NYO

Sho = all living beings, all existences.
Butsu = Buddha.
Ichi nyo = are not two.

Sentient beings and Buddha are identical, we and Buddha are the same.

At the level of satori, there is no difference. In satori there is no substance, only *ku.*

Ku soku ze shiki: Out of nothing, out of *ku,* phenomena or *shiki* arise, appear. *Ku* means without substance. Buddha has no substance. Sentient beings have no substance. So in the end they are the same.

Sho butsu ichi nyo: All sentient beings, all living existences and Buddha are one. We and Buddha, we and God, are the same, not separate, only one. There is no duality, but unity.

3. SHODEN NO BUPPO

The true transmitted Buddhism.

All other forms of Buddhism are not the true Buddhism. Without the practice of zazen there is no true Buddhism. The rest is imagination.

4. JIJUYU ZANMAI

Jijuyu = to accept or receive in oneself, by oneself.

Zanmai = samadhi, satori, the exact attention and concentration of zazen.

Samadhi is received, experienced, by oneself. Oneself alone can experience the joy of it. Other people cannot understand.

Mind and body are one. Our bodies and minds are beyond our personal egos. They are the substance of great nature, the cosmos itself. The cosmos is the unity of our bodies and minds. When we understand that, we begin the real study of Buddhism and reach the heart of religion.

16

衆佛一如

SHŌ BUTSU ICHI NYŌ

SHŌ DEN NO BUPPO

自受用三昧

JI JŪ YU ZAN MAÏ

教行證一等

KYŌ GYŌ SHŌ ITTO

No one can understand the religious joy within those who become truly intimate with themselves.

It's a form of concentration that not only doesn't create disorder in the mind but actually organizes it, that creates order within us.

Zazen means to become intimate with oneself. During zazen we follow the cosmic order naturally, automatically, unconsciously, by means of *hishiryo*—thinking without thoughts, beyond thoughts. The result of moving from thought to thought is nervous disorders; the result of moving from non-thought to non-thought is stupor. Running away, escaping from anything at all, is not good. The natural state is *hishiryo*, but moving from non-thought to non-thought sends one to sleep. Do not sleep.

If we concentrate on posture, we forget to think and the unconscious can show itself. The best way is to move from thought to non-thought, from non-thought to thought.

In the world of zazen, in the world of *ku*, there are no more eyes, nose, tongue, ears, touch, or consciousness. Everything exists unconsciously, naturally, automatically, but there is no personal thought about that existence, nothing conscious. Everything naturally follows the cosmic order. Whatever relates to the conscious mind has nothing to do with satori. The true satori comes and cannot be felt. But a master can tell if it is there.

Then no obstacle can disturb you.

Hishiryo, samadhi. Mouth closed, body not moving, posture strong and full of energy, breathing deep, thumbs horizontal. Push the sky with the top of the head, push the earth with the knees.

The original *hishiryo* consciousness is what is being thought by the cosmos when it is in harmony with the cosmic order.

Hishiryo is not a special condition of the mind, not a special state; on the contrary, it is the natural state, original thought: it rejects nothing and includes all things.

When the brain is calm, in a state of profound serenity, then the human microcosm is a perfect and harmonious image of the macrocosm. The moment our consciousness creates the slightest

法門佛向上

BUTSU KO JŌ NO HOMON

身心一如

SHIN JIN ICHI NYŌ

concept, produces the least discriminatory notion, the harmony disappears.

During zazen, by bringing our consciousness to focus on, to move inside our posture and the calm rhythm of our breathing, we allow the right harmony to occur, producing the state of *hishiryo* consciousness.

5. KYO GYO SHO ITTO

Kyo = teaching.
Gyo = practice.
Sho = satori, wisdom, understanding.
Itto = unity.
Teaching, practice, and satori do not exist separately.

6. BUTSU KOJO NO HOMON

Buddha is the ideal of the effort of our everyday lives, but we should not be too attached to it. We must be beyond Buddha. If we are too attached, we separate Buddha from ourselves and make him into some transcendent external object.

We must become the Buddha that exists in our bodies and our minds. In most religions, God is an object of faith to which people are overly attached. This is a mistake; it sets up a duality in the mind between the self and the object of faith. The unity is broken.

That does not mean that we should not respect Buddha; only we must not be dependent.

To act with a mind that is *mushotoku,* without any goal, not seeking to get anything: that is the best course.

7. SHIN JIN ICHI NYO

Body and mind are not two.
This is the secret of Soto Zen.

SHIN JIN DATSU RAKU

SHIN JIN DATSU RAKU

BODY AND MIND DROPPED AWAY

Zazen means practicing, doing what cannot be thought by our personal consciousness. True religion is not thought, it is done. So true Zen means to practice here and now—to practice eternity here and now.

Zazen means restoring the unity of Buddhahood and self, not just during zazen but in every action of everyday life. When everyday action is right, satori is being realized unconsciously, naturally, automatically.

Every day the wind rises in our human minds, creating waves. If we let go of all the illusions of our personal consciousness, we can begin to see a new life. Zazen means letting go of the education and training instilled in us from birth. *Shin jin datsu raku,* Dogen said, body and mind dropped away, metamorphosed. It isn't hard. *Shin jin datsu raku* simply means letting go of egoism. When attachment to the ego is abandoned, *shin jin datsu raku* occurs.

Only zazen is true. Everything else is the effect of karma,* the power of karma.

I don't need people's opinions. Some people say, "Please, listen, listen!" And they talk. I say nothing. It's better. People's opinions are the product of their karma. "I saw it with my own eyes, it's true. I heard it with my own ears." But those eyes and ears are not a reliable reflection of absolute truth. They are the eyes and ears of karma. That's the problem.

So we need to come back to the original condition. Zazen. If you continue to practice, your karma can diminish, although some people, even during zazen, only increase their karma. In any case, the only chance we have to forget and cut off our karma is in zazen, sitting on our zafu. Then we follow the cosmic order.

Every individual has a karma, habits, customs. That is why each person understands something different from my teaching, because they each see it through their own karma. Instead, we should hear it through *hishiryo* consciousness, without ego, without a personal consciousness. You must cut away your private categories, have empty hands and an empty head.

The power of karma is strong in everyone, stupid or clever. When that force is broken, it becomes possible to understand Zen. Most people are led, governed by their karma. They run after what they love, what attracts and impresses them.

Don't be deceived by karma. We must go ahead of time, ahead of eternity; find the world without karma.

Every morning we practice zazen. While you practice, your karma diminishes; you just sit on your zafu. That is the world without karma. During zazen, illusions and thoughts arise and

*Deshimaru Roshi uses the term *karma* in its fullest, broadest sense of "action" (of body, mouth [speech], or mind [formulated thought]); to him it almost means manifestation, and it certainly means everything that has been and everything that is now, in society, nation, family, individual. What is particularized or differentiated pertains to karma, and has all the advantages and disadvantages of that condition.

pass away. The time spent in zazen is the most precious time. ✓
During that time, suffering is reduced.

Our world is a floating world. People walk in zigzags, like drunkards, and play on the path of life and death.

Practicing zazen means making a 180-degree turn, moving from our ordinary existence to the highest holy life. Through zazen it is possible to leap directly into the holy world, the land of God or Buddha, here and now. Zazen is not the Dharma, the teaching, that makes it possible for us to live in the ordinary world; it is the Dharma, the teaching, that makes it possible for us to live in the highest world.

But even if we practice zazen, we cannot gain anything from zazen itself. Satori means losing all benefit or profit. It means taking a loss. Satori is like the mind of the thief who breaks into an empty house: nothing to steal, nothing to do. Nobody starts chasing him, and he's disappointed. Kodo Sawaki always used to say, "Zazen is like a thief breaking into an empty house."

Try it and you will understand the zazen mind. Nothing. It is not pessimism or nihilism or any "ism," it is a way of seeing that becomes the creative source of the highest wisdom.

I hope you will reach this state of mind as soon as possible; then you will find eternal freedom from life and death.

In any event, the problems of true freedom, peace, and happiness are not outside your mind; they have to do with your inner revolution through zazen. ✓

All the events in life, good or bad, sad or joyful, should be observed like a stage play, and one's inner mind should always remain at peace.

To persevere in the practice of zazen, you must feel *mujo bodai shin* very strongly.

Bodai shin = the highest spirit: spirit of awakening, mind of the way.

Mujo = impermanence.

Without that spirit of awakening, zazen becomes a competition with oneself or others, or a lifeless ritual, and one cannot

25

persevere. But if there is *bodai shin*, then the practice becomes the highest religious spirit.

The great men in history, saints and wise men, have realized that ultimately their power did not amount to much, and it was because they understood this that they became truly great and harmonized with the cosmos.

Religion means finding harmony with the cosmic system.

What you must study is the cosmic system. We do not live by or for ourselves, we are also lived by others; we are all interdependent.

Zen is zazen: meditation, the essence of religion, beyond religions and philosophies, but through the experience of the body. Concentration here and now.

The philosophy of Zen can only be understood through practice. If you want to be in good health or to have success, that is not pure Zen. Zen is only zazen. Forget everything and concentrate only on what you are doing, without any purpose. That is *mushotoku*, no profit.

During zazen you must not try to know the truth or banish your illusions. You do not think deliberately, but you are receptive to the deep unconscious, the Alaya consciousness, the reservoir of all the seeds deposited by our karma and previous actions.

Hishiryo consciousness is not a "special condition." Satori and nirvana mean the normal condition, the true, endless peace that continues after death, forever.

GYOJI

PRACTICE
EVERY DAY

———

If for one day and one night you follow the rules, the teaching of the Buddhas and patriarchs, you will see that their teachings are all the same. And if you follow those rules for a year or two, your whole life will become like that day and night.

Wanting to be different is not the best attitude. Follow the skin, flesh, bones, and marrow of the patriarchs: that is the essence of Zen.

Gyoji has nothing to do with personal effort. There is no end to *gyoji*. Repetition, for no special purpose and without end, is the way to follow the cosmic order, like the sun that gives light to the planet every day without asking anyone to pay.

Gyoji means practicing *dokan,* the ring of the way, over and over, repeating the way day after day. The point is not to look for something, but to practice.

On the great way of the Buddha and patriarchs, the highest practice, beyond all doubt, is to perpetuate *dokan*, the unending ring; to continue until you reach your coffin.

Genjo, power, comes through practice. If you practice every day, after a while you no longer have to think about practicing or decide or want to practice. So repetition is very important.

In true Buddhism, and especially in Zen, there is the notion of *muga,* non-ego, no God, no partner, no object of any sort.

If you reach a high dimension, there is no God or Buddha, while as long as you are trying to reach something there can be no high dimension. The essence of Zen is *mushotoku,* non-seeking, and no duality between God and ego. "Only practice" is the best—but without any object, without trying to achieve anything whatsoever.

In the end, even one drop of rain, falling day after day, can wear a hole in a stone.

Zazen is non-ego, *muga.* No other, no partner: harmony, complete unity with all other existences and the cosmos. In the end, we can understand that there is no need to be individualistic and self-centered. Being one with everybody else becomes what gives us happiness.

You are living Buddhas, living gods. Your zazen posture itself is holy, is God, Buddha. Buddha, God, and the saints do not exist here and now. But living divinity, living Buddhahood, living holiness exists in you. Through the merits of *dokan,* here and now, the spirit of Buddha is transformed into activity.

Because of this, the true way is not interrupted. *Dokan* continues forever and Buddha remains beyond Buddha. The spirit of Buddha is always present. Buddha is always perfect, and true satori happens.

Descartes said, "I think, therefore I am." Dogen said, "I practice, therefore I am; I exist here, I act here."

If you continue *gyoji* faithfully, great merits will follow. But gaining merits cannot be the objective; that must be simply to continue zazen.

One day the Buddha Shakyamuni was preaching and at the end he said, "Do not run after a man or a woman; it is better to look into yourself."

The internal revolution is important, but hard:

> *A man always remains a man.*
> *A man congeals like a man.*
> *A woman congeals like a woman.*
> *An intellectual congeals like an intellectual.*
> *A madman congeals like a madman.*

This congealing, inflexibility, is the cause of many troubles. But once it is finished, once the personality becomes straight and honest and a person joins the cosmic order, then the mind grows soft and supple and there is no longer any reason to hide or run away from anything. The mind, the spirit, is always shining, sparkling, day after day. That is sainthood. The quality is straight, the consciousness unresisting. That is the essential point of Dogen's Zen. Sky and earth have the same body, all existences have the same root. No need to create a separation between myself and others. When you let go of the "isms," the solidified, congealed thoughts, then you can find true satori, true *do,* the Tao (the Way).

The wise, the holy, have no ego; everything becomes their ego. The sky, the earth, and I have the same root; all existences and I myself form but one body.

You will gain nothing by trying to climb higher than other people. Wanting to be different is harmful.

Just practice zazen, stay quiet. Do not bother with people who sneer and call you dumb because you do not speak. That is their mistake. Through *shikantaza* you become Buddha—not the historic Buddha who lived 2,500 years ago, but living Buddhas, living Bodhidharmas, living Christs. Zazen is the greatest and most holy of postures. Through it you become the link that joins sky to earth. Practice *shin jin datsu raku* * and your body and mind are transformed.

Do not congeal. Do not become a bigot or a fanatic. To congeal makes the mind brittle and small. It is written in the *Shodoka* †: Walking, sitting, standing, lying down, speaking, remaining silent: all are Zen.

When you live with other people, the group becomes a mirror.

We need to learn about the *gyoji* of the patriarchs of old and imitate their spirit. Life then was not the same as it is now, and every person is different too, but the spirit is always the same. We must understand and repeat, over and over.

Practice must not be beyond consciousness, and consciousness must not be beyond practice. Practice and consciousness must always be identical. Practice must follow consciousness, and consciousness must follow practice. The body's practice and the awareness in the consciousness must be one.

True wisdom cannot be shut up inside categories. It is a creation that takes place here and now, infinite and eternal. The great wise man lives in the street, the small one goes off to the mountain.

In the streets of Paris or New York it is possible to be wise. In our temple at La Gendronnière, the stables have become a dojo. In other places, churches have been turned into theaters or music halls. There is nothing particular to say about places, one place or another. Do not cling to your family or birthplace. If you feel gratitude or love for your family, cut yourself free from that feeling. If you receive gifts, do not cling to them. If you receive land, do not cling to it. If you have children, do not cling to them. But if you are alone and have nothing, do not cling to that, either.

Since the beginning, since prehistoric times, we have reproduced the worst in ourselves, over and over again. In fact, we know quite well what is good and what is bad, but we act as though we were putting our feet where our heads should go. The

Shin jin datsu raku = body and mind dropped away; see previous chapter.
†"Song of Immediate Satori," by Yoka, seventh-century Chinese.

30

result is that we suffer and long for things. If we do not cut off our desires here and now, when can we end them? If we do not practice here and now, when can we practice the true *gyoji?*

For the way, practicing *gyoji* is enough. If you do not accept this, you will waste your time for all eternity.

We can act and be acted by *gyoji.* That is why the body that practices *gyoji* is sacred and holy, and so is the mind. We should not let them become impure. They are not a personal body or a personal mind.

Our life: What is life? What? Why do we exist? That is a philosophical question. In Buddhism, and especially in Zen, what matters is how we behave, how we live. It is not necessary to study metaphysics. Most religions want to analyze, discover the substance of God and the substance of the ego, the self. Buddhism has nothing to say on this subject.

What matters in Buddhism is behavior, what one does and how one does it. There is no rejection of metaphysical questions, but nothing is said about them in the commentaries. As in other religions, moral precepts are important. But in Zen, however important the precepts may be, they are based on practice, because by continuing zazen we are necessarily obeying the precepts, unconsciously and automatically.

> The precepts are the sword of non-fearing that draws the venom from the poison of our wrongdoing. The precepts are the last companion, the ultimate friend who helps us over the hidden ruts and snares in the way. The precepts are the gateway to the exquisite nectar where the wise play freely together. To protect the precepts means not to glorify oneself; it means to embrace what is refined, to shun what is base. If you do not imprison the just precept, by calling it this or that, no error will be created.

Gyoji (constant practice) and *setsu* (sermons, teaching, understanding, intellect) relate to each other like water and waves. They are like the two wings of a bird. If one wing is damaged the bird cannot fly. Both are necessary.

31

Gyoji is like summer. If you concentrate here and now on each action, then in the autumn the harvest will come. You do not need to look forward to it. If you concentrate here and now on *gyoji,* a great harvest will come that you can store over the winter, and then spring will come again. That is *gyoji, dokan,* like a wheel. The circle, the ring of the way.

Gyoji has no end. It is infinite. The ring of the way that goes on eternally. If everyone practiced it, the country would prosper for one thousand autumns and pass on its benefits through ten thousand generations.

THE
SPIRIT
OF ZEN

There is light in the darkness;
Do not look with dark-seeing eyes.
There is darkness in the light;
Do not look with light-seeing eyes.

KO MYŌ ZŌ ZAN MAÏ

KOMYOZO ZANMAI

THE SAMADHI
OF THE STOREHOUSE
OF GREAT WISDOM

Komyo means light, illumination.

Zo is the attic, storehouse, granary.

Zanmai is samadhi or *hishiryo* consciousness.

The following twelve paragraphs are part of a text written "with deepest respect" by Ejo—the longtime personal secretary of Dogen, founder of Soto Zen in Japan—at the temple of Eiheiji, on August 28, 1278, "in the reign of Guta." All masters since, including Deshimaru Roshi, have made commentaries on it.

Do not try to experience satori. Do not try to drive away illusion. Do not hate the thoughts that arise, and do not love them either; above all, do not *entertain* them. Just practice the great sitting, here and now. If you do not continue a thought, it will not come back of its own accord. If you let yourself go in your own breathing-out, if you let your breath-

Zen - thoughts vs thinking

ing-in fill you in a harmonious coming and going, all that remains is a zafu under an empty sky, the weight of a flame.

If you do not expect anything from what you do, if you refuse to consider anything whatsoever, you can cut everything by zazen alone.

Even if eighty-four thousand illusions come and go, if you do not attach any importance to them and let them make their own way, the wonderful mystery of the storehouse of great wisdom can leap up from every one of them.

There is not just the *komyo,* illumination, of the time during zazen. There is also the light that gradually leads you, step by step, act after act, to see that everything can be realized immediately, without passing through your intelligence and your thoughts.

In the hour of your birth, *komyo* did not exist. In the hour of your death, it will not disappear.

Buddhas do not have more of it; sentient beings do not have less.

When you have illusions or doubts, you cannot ask the right question, and when you have satori, you cannot express it. Moment by moment, consider nothing with your personal consciousness. Twenty-four hours out of twenty-four, you should be as calm, as vastly tranquil as the dead. Think of nothing on your own. This way, breathing out and breathing in, both your deepest nature and your sentient nature will become, unconsciously, non-knowing, non-understanding.

Then, naturally, everything can become the calm radiance of *komyo,* in oneness of mind and body. Therefore, when there is a call, the answer must come quickly. One and the same *komyo* harmonizes both enlightened and deluded people into one whole. Even if you move, the movement should not disturb. Forest, flowers, blades of grass, animals, people, all phenomena, long or short, square or round, can be realized immediately, automatically, without any action by the individual intelligence and independently of the mind or will.

Do not care about clothes or food or a home. Do not give way to sensual desire or the attachment of love, for that is what animals do.

Also, it is useless to ask other people about *komyo*, because their *komyo* can be no use to you at all.

Before time began, this samadhi was the holy dojo, like the ocean of all the Buddhas. It is the greatest and most holy of all sittings, transmitted directly from Buddha to Buddha through the universal practice of zazen. Now, being disciples of Buddha yourselves, you should practice zazen peacefully in his seat.

Do not sit on the cushion of hell, the *gaki*, animal or *asura* cushion, or even on the cushion of the *shomon* or *engaku*.* Practice nothing but *shikantaza*. Do not waste time. That is what is known as the true spirit of the dojo and the true *komyozo* samadhi, wonderful and splendid freedom.

In the *Shodoka*, Yoka says, "There is nothing to find in the world of satori, no person, not even Buddha. The innumerable cosmoses themselves are like bubbles in the ocean. All the wisest and most venerable people are like streaks of lightning in the sky."

The brilliance of *komyozo zanmai* is everywhere, in every mind, everywhere in the cosmos. We must believe it. It has nothing to do with any particular, individual illumination. Our mind must be the storehouse, the granary of that divine light. We must have faith in this illumination, which has no special substance situated in any particular place in the cosmos.

The fundamental essence of *komyozo zanmai* is *mushotoku*, unremitting effort. Unremitting effort does not mean choosing or abandoning oneself to samadhi only. Do not prefer *ku*, the void, on the pretext that *shiki*, things, should be rejected. This is a religious problem, not a social problem.

When you have understood this, your mind will reflect gen-

*In some traditions, there are different "levels" of meditation ranging from the infernal to the beatific and beyond, and passing by the levels of *gaki*—starving, roving spirits—*asura*, *shomon*, and *engaku*, which are other levels of realization.

tleness and compassion. A sense of conviction comes, but without any act of will, and you harmonize with all existences, creating more and more infinite beauty. This is the true *komyozo*, shining out in our resolution.

It has nothing to do with what you show other people. It is secret. True religion is like that.

HŌ KYŌ ZAN MAÏ

HOKYO
ZANMAI

THE MIRROR SAMADHI

During a talk one day, the Buddha Shakyamuni picked up a flower and turned it gently in his fingers. None of the disciples gathered around him understood his gesture; only Mahakashyapa smiled. So the Buddha said to him:

"The secret of nirvana, my wonderful secret, you alone have realized it and I give it to you now."

That is the samadhi of the spirit of Buddha, the Buddha-mind.

The Buddha-mind is like a mirror, and the mind of Mahakashyapa was reflected in it. The reflected image was a perfectly pure spirit, original mind, in perfect and total unity with the mind of the Buddha. The Buddha was the mirror. Mahakashyapa's mind entered the mirror. Only karma, only Mahakashyapa's form, was looking at the mirror; but what the mirror reflected was not

Mahakashyapa, it was original mind, pure and at one with the mind of Buddha and the light of Buddha.

Mahakashyapa's reflection had become Buddha. Looking at the Buddha's mind, Mahakashyapa was looking at his own mind, and he understood this.

The image in the mirror is you
but you are not the image.

Your existence is not the mirror-image. When we look into the mirror, the mirror does not make the reflection by itself and it cannot grasp the form. The combination of the two is necessary. Even if there is a mirror, you cannot see the reflection unless you look into it.

The relationship among consciousness, wisdom, and the cosmos is the same as that among mirror, reflection, and form.

Never, as long as we live, can we see our own face. All we know is the reflection in the mirror; we never see ourselves directly. We have to have the intermediary, the reflection in the mirror. But the mirror is not truth, only a mirror.

Five hundred monkeys were looking at the moon's reflection in the water and thinking, "What a gorgeous melon, let's go pick it." All together, from valley to lake they went, holding each other's hands to make a chain, trying to pick the wonderful moon-melon mirrored in the water, and every last one of them fell in the lake.

It is like trying to put the sky in a bucket, trying to catch the wind and tie it up in a rope. That is typical of our civilization, and that is why it says in the *Shodoka* that you must not try to catch the moon in a bucket or the wind in the sky.

During zazen we have illusions produced by our five senses —colors, voices, smells, tastes, touch. But we shouldn't worry about them, because samadhi, mirror concentration, remains perfectly untainted.

We must not separate *shiki* from *ku*, phenomenon from essence; instead, we must just let go of both, not only *shiki* but *ku* as well.

42

We must not make categories. In everyday life, in our arguments, it is always, "I'm right and you're wrong." We always want to compare and compete with each other. So in the sutras—the *Nirvana Sutra,* the *Lotus Sutra,* the *Diamond Cutter Sutra*—the Zen monk speaks with a boneless tongue. That means he must speak in every direction, embrace every contradiction, without resistance.

PENETRATE OUR TRUE NATURE

We must create continuously, but out of what?

We must create, make new, out of the heart of tradition.

We must find the essence, *ku,* but if we want to find the true *ku* we must find phenomena too.

We must not be defined by past history or our present life in society.

We must not ignore past history or our present life in society.

Zazen means penetrating the most total solitude of the human being.

A person alone can become closely acquainted with himself and herself, can achieve profound intimacy, and in that way can reach the true self.

Our life is the voyage of solitude.
A strong, true person, brave and great,
Does not need help from others,
Has no wish for it.

We must become our true nature,
We must find our way into that true nature,
Walking firmly on the path.
There is only my one self,
There is no second self beneath myself.

If we achieve satori and the satori shows, like a bit of dogshit stuck on the tip of our nose, that is not so good.

If we are kind and nice to everybody, and our niceness sticks out on the tip of our nose, it will not be real niceness.

Most of the time people want to hide their bad sides and show only the good.

Sometimes *ku*, sometimes *shiki*: this is better.

We must not be dependent upon anything whatever. Like the farmer working in his field, facing the sun as it comes up: dependent on nothing, neither illusions nor satori. He's all farmer. Nothing bothers him.

Restrictions are illusions. They mean: we restrict ourselves.

For example: I don't like, I hate, I love, I want honors, I want money. I want to go somewhere, I want to travel.

Those are all desires, illusions. Desires govern our everyday lives, and the result is suffering, discomfort, dissatisfaction.

These are dependencies.

Buddha means true freedom.

Zazen is true freedom.

One night a thief crept into a little hermitage and found nothing he could steal. But he saw Ryokan asleep in his blanket. So the thief snatched the blanket and ran away. The cold woke Ryokan, who sneezed and saw that his blanket had been stolen.

The moon was shining, magnificent in the sky, and Ryokan could see it from his window. He then wrote a famous poem.

Oh, wonderful!
So lovely, the moon in my window!
Why did the thief not take it too?

No event could upset his peace of mind.

The moonlight shines on every blade of grass. That is a universal cosmic phenomenon, it is the nature of Buddha, God, it fills the whole cosmos. So we can breathe, observe the whole cosmos, hear every sound in the cosmos, smell and taste every flavor and forest. We must touch the whole cosmos. That is true zazen. *Shikantaza.*

But even if we think we have understood everything, even if we study the highest philosophy, if we do not put it into practice, if all the profit we derive from it is for ourselves, then that is no true religion, no true philosophy.

We must never stop progressing. Always take one more step. If we do that, then the whole cosmos becomes our body. If we let go of the little ego, the whole cosmos becomes ego. Taking one more step, you are surely alive but as though dead; you die to yourself. Letting go of the ego again and again, you can become free. There is no cul-de-sac.

Sitting in zazen is like fishing the moonlight and plowing the clouds. The mind opens wide, everything grows calm, you can become close to yourself.

In religions, people ask God or Buddha for things. In Zen, they talk to themselves.

We always go alone. The way of practice is profoundly solitary. Even deep love for someone else cannot destroy the aloneness. Husband and wife in the same bed do not dream the same dreams.

What makes Zen exist is practice, repetition of practice. Even if you have understood all the good zazen can do, it is hard to keep practicing. If you continue, you have a priceless treasure, because you are following the cosmic order.

The way is one. The way up and the way down are the same. They are the same way, but the starting-point differs. When

Buddha Shakyamuni was climbing up the mountain he was filled with a great hope, but he came back down exhausted, his body worn and broken. The way up is the way to satori, the way down is the way of salvation, the way of compassion, but they are inseparable; beyond their duality they are one.

Sitting in zazen is satori, truth. Zazen itself is satori, the way up the mountain. But zazen is also the way down.

Our attitude must be exact, fearless, firm. It must be like a blow, a spark; that is the true attitude of zazen.

In part it is resolution, a strong posture, and in part it is delicate, elegant, like the scent of sandalwood or incense.

When each consciousness perseveres, through constant changes, in the same thought, that thought unconsciously becomes real.

In the end, you must not try to reach any goal; only then do you reach it truly, only then does it become unconsciously real.

MU SHŌ TOKU

MUSHOTOKU

NO GOAL OR
DESIRE FOR GAIN

Having even one goal, even the tiniest preference or the most infinitesimal thought, or pursuing some objective, however feeble, automatically and inevitably drives us away from the truth of zazen. A man may think that by becoming a monk and respecting the precepts, by following a rigorous practice, he is practicing Buddhism, but if he still has the slightest goal he will heap error upon error and sink into mortification or self-centeredness or, at the least, dogmatism.

Satori means nothing more than to become *mushotoku* and understand *mushotoku* intimately and deeply.

Kodo Sawaki used to say that satori was like total damage, absolute loss—in other words, the nakedness of the self, death of the self, extinction of the self and any quest.

Annihilating the attached mind, adhering to nothing, expecting nothing, chasing nothing, wanting nothing: that is *mushotoku*.

People are forever calculating and counting, more, less. . . .
But in Zen, if you give something to somebody, if there is a gift,
you must forget to whom it was given, who gave it, and what it
was. The action should have no object.

What is a true gift? When nothing is expected in return.

In the end, you give a sense of safety, confidence, relief by
giving your body, face, words. That is what a real gift should be
like, expecting nothing in return.

If you long to savor some delicious dish and do not touch it,
that becomes a great gift for mankind and the whole world, its
merits are boundless. A gift is not necessarily a physical object.
The sublimation of desires is a perfect gift.

People are always calculating, always pursuing some objective. But *mushotoku* has no objective. Mind has no fetters. Freedom is not the same thing as egoism. Attaching too much
importance to oneself is not freedom. And it leads to much
trouble and many difficulties. If you are self-centered in your
relations with others, you will have trouble.

But if the mind follows only the cosmic order, if it becomes
mushotoku, you are no longer afraid of anything. If the mind does
not stick to anything, does not grasp anything, then there is no
need to be afraid.

Mushotoku = total abandonment of self, thoughts, goals,
the whole mental structure that is the foundation for the development of the ego. True compassion is this abandonment; it begins
with it and ends with it.

Do not try to make conscious thoughts apply to the realm
of wisdom, and do not try to achieve wisdom; because true wisdom is *mushotoku.* It can be obtained only unconsciously, naturally, automatically. It transcends all limitations created by the
mind. It is immediately beyond space-time, eternal, immutable.

Ultimately, the highest wisdom is objectless, without consciousness. It is *mushotoku.* It does not arise in the forebrain but
in the thalamus, the central brain, and it is born out of the whole
body. That is perfect wisdom.

THE MIDDLE
WAY

—

Zen Buddhism is not all spiritual and it is not all material; it embraces both.

Nowadays, harmony between the two is hard to achieve. Some people see everything in terms of mind or spirit, others think that nothing is true unless you can touch it, and there is no link between the two. What we must find is the middle way, leaning neither to one side nor to the other. *Buddha* means the middle way, balance. But the middle way does not mean being halfway between one thing and another. It includes both aspects, good and evil, feminine and masculine, most and least.

All existences are *ku*, impermanent, changing, lacking any permanent substance; the only thing that exists in the world of phenomena is perpetual change. The ego has no substance of its own, is not an entity, and has no autonomy; it is simply the momentary actualization of a set of interdependent causes that, together, possessing potentiality, can form the fabric of phenomena. There is no real substance in body or mind; their substance is possibility, the virtuality of existence, the potential of manifestation; and it is this very quality, this potentiality, that is the fundamental cosmic power itself.

It is a rare virtue to be able to distinguish truth from lies; a smile, a kind word, and we automatically respond, but without really being able to tell the difference between true kindness and hypocrisy. How can we go beyond the words to the heart of a thought that does not say its name? How can we see the real face that wears a smile for a mask? Our inability to tell the difference is a weakness. We like to content ourselves with superficialities, rather than dig down to authenticity—because what it reveals is not always comforting to the ego.

If you want to perceive reality, you must not indulge the weakness of choosing between what is pleasant and what is unpleasant; you must start in the state of *hishiryo*, free from any notion of agreeable or disagreeable.

Some people like change, so they also like a constant change of spiritual practice; they jump from one to another without ever finding satisfaction anywhere; they wander, lost, until they die. They lack the strength to persevere and be patient, and above all they do not understand being without an objective, not being attached to the idea of getting something. If you really want to get to the top of the mountain you must follow a single path and stick to it, dig and slog till your body is used up and abandoned, till your mind is used up and dropped behind.

True satori is in us. There's no need to look for it anywhere else, or to change masters.

Everything is a shining pearl, even the cavern of the demon of the black mountain. The cavern of the demon of the black mountain means the illusions engendered by thought, by the subject/object split, by duality. In most people today the brain is the cavern of the demon of the black mountain. Our unending human struggle to escape, to get out of hell, has become even more desperate today, because our civilization has turned down a dead-end road.

Gensha's statement that the whole universe is a shining pearl means that the universe cannot be and is not limited by such concepts as great or small, wide or narrow, square or round, nor by the center, the macro- or micro-; when all these forms are transcended, the universe itself emerges. There is neither life nor death, neither going nor remaining, but only the changes themselves, which are the very life of the Buddhas, the materialization of truth. That is why the past is gone and the present actualizes itself. As to ultimate meaning—who can confine it to the unending movement of life and death on one side, and immobility on the other?

All differentiation ceases between cosmos as object and ego as subject, yet the cosmos is still the cosmos and the ego still the ego.

The pearl image is directly related to eternity; time past and time present are both part of eternity, and therefore have no end. The cosmos and the whole universe are a shining pearl. Our bodies exist in reality; so do our reason and our intellect. But no object exists individually, in itself, as an entity—blade of grass, tree, mountain, sky, or earth. Everything is only a shining pearl.

There is no escape, no way out of the universe, which is nothing but a shining pearl. Even if you believe you have escaped for a split second, you are still in time, and time is covered by the shining pearl.

A shining pearl is the whole universe; the cavern of the demon of the black mountain is also a shining pearl. Our illusions are changed into satori, just as the cavern of the demon of the black mountain becomes the shining pearl of the whole universe.

Our minds are constantly in motion, they are often the cavern of the demon of the black mountain. Most people alive today are in hell; they suffer, so they make plans and dream of a better future. But now is when they must act, to transmute the hell into a shining pearl.

Not by riding the thief's horse, however, which is what most people do. You cannot free yourself from the hell of discomfort and frustration by throwing fuel on the flames of desire. People want to be free and yet stay in hell.

Mahayana Buddhism has always refuted dualism as a product of our mental structure, which is limited by space-time, and has preached the unity of all things, which can be achieved by transcending thought through the practical method of *hishiryo* meditation.

In the realm of phenomena, which cannot be disassociated from the realm of the absolute, the law of causality that governs all things manifested is precisely the other face of the absolute freedom on which the cosmic potential is based: one sheet of paper, with causality and things on one side, freedom and potential on the other; but only one sheet of paper.

The narrower our understanding, the stronger the influence of the law of causality in producing the karmas of body, speech, and mind. The broader our understanding, the greater our freedom, opening into the potentiality of infinite action. With this sort of freedom, true freedom, past karma comes to an end, and a potential for action is released and expressed in absolutely appropriate phenomena.

The practice of zazen gives rise to the infinite potential act that reverberates here and now throughout the cosmos, and that act is perpetuated for eternity. In other words, eternity is actualized in the here-and-now of every act.

The shining pearl is the eye of the true Dharma, the body of truth, the body of the eternal, universal truth. The pearl shines more or less brightly as we move forward or backward inside the cavern of the demon of the black mountain. But whether we enter or leave, the pearl remains. Its brilliance can be seen only in the light, though, when the boulders of the cavern walls have split apart and fallen away.

THE BRIGHTER
THE LIGHT,
THE DEEPER
THE SHADOW

THE INTERDEPENDENCE
OF PHENOMENA

What directs the cosmos? What is cosmic order? Every star is related to and dependent upon every other star. Energy makes the whole universe move. On this earth we are like mushrooms.

Body and brain are built on the same principles as the cosmos. Thoughts fly up to the sky like soap bubbles that burst and return to the cosmos. So it is with our lives. What is important is to control and observe. Keep control of the self, observe that in the heart of the fiercest winter the spring is already there.

When the snow falls, the plum tree is already budding.

All existences are interdependent. We have no separate substance; all the body's organs, liver, spleen, lungs, sexual organs, live together; and there is a direct connection between body and mind. If the body is in good condition, the mind is right too. So good posture and right breathing lead to a return to a normal condition of the brain.

Engi, the law of causes and effects, of interdependence, governs all things; it is the fabric of every existence.

BODY-MIND
IS ONE

The Buddha way is not studied in somebody else, or in any outside ⌐ ✓
place, but in one's own body-mind.

Back in the thirteenth century, Dogen wrote that it was
possible to think with the body, a notion now being confirmed by
science. The great Oriental masters knew these things intuitively
and transmitted them to their disciples. Nowadays, psychologists
and physiologists are investigating Zen, although most of the time
they do not want to practice themselves, so they cannot really
understand.

You who practice are precious, and your experience of coming here every day will prove essential.

Zazen is *shin jin datsu raku.*

Shin jin = body and mind.

Datsu = take off, remove, shed.

Raku = throw away.

Body and mind are completely stripped; but it's not the same as the snake shedding its skin. It is exactly the point at which ego and Buddha touch, ego and all existences meet, and the point itself disappears. It is samadhi.

To be intelligent, to understand, to learn, is also important. But it is even more important to control, to regulate, mind and body.

Intelligence and book-learning are not first conditions. Cerebral knowledge and activity are not first conditions. True masters throughout the past have avoided them and reached the Buddha's way by gaining control over their own bodies and minds.

For Dogen, action comes before thought. That is a basic principle of the martial arts. In a kendo match, for example, the antagonists' survival or death depends upon the swiftness, the instantaneity, of their movements. The action is born and operates from within, prompted by unmediated intuition and accompanied by no discursive thought.

Very often, thought and action are disassociated. The body doesn't follow, there is no outcome, nothing happens. That is a symptom of depression, of the sort of fatigue that is becoming so persistent a feature of our type of civilization.

The state of samadhi is the penetration of the fundamental cosmic power into every part of the body during zazen. The actions of our everyday lives must reflect that state. And those actions are necessary for the state of samadhi to become manifest.

When body and mind are one and in perfect harmony, a condition that you can understand during zazen, samadhi is manifested, the true Buddha way is manifested. There is no further differentiation between the object of knowledge and the subject that knows. When this happens, both particularized aspects—both stillness and motion—cease utterly. That is the meaning of the words "to master": to gain control over mind and body.

The mind is like a rider on a horse, the body is the horse, and the relationship of body to mind is the same as that of horse to rider. A great koan says, "No rider in the saddle, no horse under the saddle."

In *hishiryo* consciousness there is no illusion or attachment.
It is just like the clouds rising from the mountain, or the reflection
of the moon on the stream in the valley.

> *The moon is me, I am the moon.*
> *Which is moon? Which is me?*
> *No way to tell them apart.*
> *My mind and this moon have flowed together.*
> *This night's moon has cleaned my mind*
> *Just as it has cleaned the sky.*

Dogen's Zen does not consist in experiencing satori. Between me and Buddha, between God and myself, there is no more
touching point, no more dividing line. Buddha is in self, self is in
Buddha. The whole cosmos enters me. I enter the whole cosmos.
Subject and object interpenetrate. That is samadhi. Attachment
to ego ends.

It is not possible to experience satori through the brain, the
consciousness. Dogen explains that it must be experienced
through the body.

When, during zazen, you abandon your narrow, personal
consciousness, your personal body and mind, when you forget
your pseudo-wisdom, exactly then can you realize cosmic wisdom
fully.

KARMA
AND SELF

———

What is the fundamental force called karma?

It does not operate only in the human world, but subtends the whole cosmos; it governs all existences, nature, the whole earth, and all the galaxies; it supports, directs, and orders everything.

The cosmos is never at rest. It assembles and destroys, producing order and chaos at once.

The cosmic energy that fills and influences the whole universe and all existences throughout eternity, by which all nature is impregnated, from minerals and plants to sentient beings, animals and humans, is taken in, absorbed by every individual existence unconsciously, naturally, and automatically. During zazen you can understand the form and force of the energy called karma, feel and recognize it unconsciously, naturally, automatically, through *hishiryo* consciousness.

60

It is possible to intervene deliberately in your karma and change it. A human being is not a definitively structured, rigid organism. It is in constant evolution, and its evolutionary structure explains its flexibility and ability to adapt to new circumstances. Multiple possibilities are open to it, ranging from obstinate rigidity and ego-affirmation to complete adaptability and flexibility or ego-abandonment.

There is something deterministic, irrevocable, and mysterious about fate or destiny, but not so with karma, in which the rigorous necessity of causality, the necessity that we understand as a characteristic of destiny, is attenuated because our lives are a composite whole and cannot be ruled by the principle of causality alone. There are many antecedents, many prior causes, and they do not systematically produce a single, inevitable result. The activity of the psyche is partly conditioned by these antecedents, beyond any doubt, but it is not totally determined by them.

The human consciousness has developed the concept of voluntary choice, a lucidly weighed option, a possibility that is not inevitable. In the lower orders of nature, the realm of minerals, plants, and animals, phenomena are governed by strict necessity alone, the physical law of determinism. If the required conditions are present, the phenomenon appears. But the determinism of the principle of causality can have no absolute power over the human psyche. The more a person wakes up to reality and understands it, the less influence determinism will have upon that person and the greater will be his or her freedom of action, autonomy, unpredictability.

Our life is an actualization of a long evolution originating in the night of time. It takes place in time, but it is a perpetual transformation in which there is a part that is relatively unvarying, and it is this that characterizes the individual: an individual goes on being himself or herself, but is never the same.

Your concentration during zazen is exactly like a snake wriggling into a bamboo pole: as long as it is inside, its body is straight, but the moment it emerges and comes into contact with the environment, it starts bending and crawling and twisting again, curving from side to side, just as we do when we emerge from our observation during zazen, and the illusions of our bad karma begin to stir again; it grows and spreads like a sheet of water that will cover the entire earth if it encounters no obstacle to stop it.

Illusions are born of desire, which engenders all the diseases of body and mind. Neuroses are the expression of a disproportion between desires and their satisfaction. If we concentrate here and now, however, our desires immediately vanish; a desire is born and dies, it goes past without affecting, without leaving any trace. Memories and plans should be the motor for action in the present, they are as essential to life as air; but if we are to be sane, they must not remain fixed or static. Everything changes, passes, and is transformed. What life means is not being fixed. An unmoving memory, like an obsessive desire, is a cancerous cell. It atrophies life, prevents the current of cosmic energy from circulating.

Sometimes we judge and understand things with the mind's eye, by intuition, without looking. Karma and illusions have become the very basis of most people's personalities, however; they have been unable to observe and regulate and go beyond them, so that the attributes of karma have become their actual characteristics. This is a serious matter.

Crazy people do not realize that they are crazy; if they did, they could be cured. In the same way, imagining one has satori is another kind of being crazy. If you possess true Zen, you cannot at the same time possess social profit or honors, and on the other hand, if you do not possess true Zen, your mind will not be in a normal condition and all you will do is accumulate more and more bad karma. The actions of present karma realize past karma, and the actions of past karma are actualized in the effects of present and future karma.

Freedom beyond time and space is a mystical experience. In our actual, social world there is only the reality of our will, profoundly limited by space. Realizing that is what is meant by waking up in regard to karma, interdependence.

The soul is infinite. We must wake up to the fact that the

self is the realization of the fundamental cosmic power. Karma is infinite. The ego is one among all existences. It consists in a relationship of interdependence with all existences.

If, during zazen, our mind stops and fastens itself to something, to any external state, we must lay hold of that mind and bring it back to right consciousness.

When the cloud follows the wind, it moves. Mind is like the cloud. It is always being led around by the devil of karma, it keeps moving constantly.

The wind of karma, the devil, directs and upsets the mind. As long as that is so, it is not free from birth and death.

ILLUSION = SATORI

The beautiful lotus flower does not grow in lush green meadows or on lofty mountain crags; it takes root in a muddy pond. We cannot obtain the treasure of absolute wisdom without entering the ocean of illusion.

Buddha and the devil have the same face. In the end, people who produce illusion have as much satori as do people who experience satori and produce satori but must return to illusion again to mingle with the creatures of illusion.

The satori person must harmonize with the person who generates only illusion, must mingle with dirt, and must leave no odor of satori behind. The satori person must come to the level of other people, drink, laugh, eat with them.

You do not need to entertain any illusion in order to be in a state of illusion, and you do not need to experience satori in order to produce satori. There can be no desire or will in this at all.

Our sins become the substance of our virtues; it is just like the relationship between ice and water.

The true great way cannot be encompassed in the notion of satori; it must be practiced profoundly, but it must not be sought.

Through wisdom, we must cut off the roots of illusions and desires at their source. But we must not forget that the illusions of our own minds produce satori; so our desires themselves become the water of satori.

The greater the volume occupied by those desires, the more abundant will be the water of satori.

When our bad karma is active, our observation is dispersed and blotted out and our good karma can no longer make itself felt.

If a person practices zazen only one hour, even a few minutes, during that time the three karmas of speech, body, and consciousness become, literally, Buddha. Because in zazen you do not speak, your body is in the highest posture, like that of Buddha, and your consciousness is *hishiryo*. That is the highest karma. At that time you are in the state of samadhi, you are like Buddha.

The true Mahayana bodhisattva does not want to cut or exorcise illusions and desires. The bodhisattva must have the courage to face life and death.

You must leap into the racing torrent, into modern civilization, not run away and hide in the mountain. Nirvana is the mountain; you must go to it and come back again.

If you face life and death with courage, then you are born as non-born and your mind cannot be totally clouded; you are like the lotus flower rooted in slime, or the physician who heals the patient without catching the disease. Like a bird that flies in the sky but does not dwell in any part of the sky.

So you must go to nirvana without cutting off desires, and purify the root of illusion without having to sever illusions.

Making choices is not good; too much choosing is an obstacle to satori. Too much choosing is a mistake, deciding "This is good, that is bad. . . ." Good can turn into evil and evil can become good. Good and evil are relative; they depend on time and circumstance.

Our life does not exist in time. But in our life, time exists. Time exists only through our practice in our everyday life. The capacity of our own will is very limited. Effort is important, of course, but we cannot make any lasting, durable headway by means of effort. Our own personal effort is limited by time and space. So we must abandon our own will, abandon the ego. Then we can be moved by the wonderful fundamental power of the cosmos.

Illusions glitter like diamonds, and people are drawn to them; illusions are what make human beings live, they are as necessary to us as air, because the end of illusion, the disappearance of phenomena, means the end of activity, the end of life, death.

The desires you observe in other people exist in your own mind too. Everything exists in your mind.

Contradictions are built into our brain. It is extremely hard to abandon the demon and keep only the saint in our brain. That way, no true satori is possible. We must not cut off our illusions. We must find satori among them.

Listening, thinking, and practicing, it is possible to enter samadhi. To be in samadhi means to be beyond illusions or saintliness, experiencing our inner purity through the body and not just through thought. It is very important to practice. Samadhi is an experience that you have alone, by yourself.

Satori is like the moon's reflection on the water: the moon does not get wet and no waves appear on the surface of the water. The moonlight illuminates infinitely, illuminates the whole earth, but can also be contained entirely in a tiny drop of water. The moonlight does not disturb the water; in the same way, do not consider satori as an obstacle to your practice.

When the light of our wisdom is turned off, the illusions of darkness appear. But the true light of wisdom of the middle way is always there; it does not move. It is like a mysterious jewel, glowing steadily.

The darkness of illusions is the light of great wisdom.

Without illusion, there is no mankind. What is bad is excess; people become like animals. How to control, to regulate; that is what matters. The key is, do not become attached. Being attached means thinking all the time about the same thing.

When cosmic energy assumes the form of phenomena it undergoes change, but its totality does not become more or less. When you obtain one thing you lose another thing. Misery turns into happiness and vice versa. Illusions become satori, *bonno soku bodai*. Everything works that way.

In the state of Buddhahood there is no more increase or decrease. It is the totality of the ten thousand phenomena, *fukatoku*—ungraspable. It is the greatest freedom, true spirituality.

You cannot grasp the air. You cannot isolate one part of it. You cannot apprehend it. Or the sky. They are *fukatoku*. Just as it is not possible to grasp your own mind. The mind is infinite, limitless. We always want to make categories, but consciousness stretches to infinity. It is *hishiryo*.

Cosmic truth is only one. It has existed forever, since before history, before human beings. Cosmic truth and the cosmic order were around before the earth. They are actualized, they give birth to phenomena of all kinds, and they assume different aspects.

The wind is invisible, but you can hear it. An inaudible sound does not exist, but you can feel it. A deaf man's ear, wind in pine trees.

If you hear nothing, then you can hear eternal sound, see invisible colors, hear the silent voice, the invisible form, the eternal, invisible, infinite consciousness. If you do not listen to complicated words and noises, you can hear the voice of eternity.

The cosmic order has nothing to do with power. It is beyond the temporal, it is the Dharma. If you follow the Dharma, your karma will change and you will know happiness.

67

Satori is the satori of practice, and so there is no end to satori. Zazen is the practice of satori, and so there is no beginning to practice.

In Mahayana Buddhism,* the Buddha's satori is not only for himself; he acts so that other people may know it too. Otherwise, satori would be completely selfish. Before your own satori, see that other people experience it first.

Wisdom is like a stout boat, a seaworthy ship crossing the ocean, the sea of suffering and death. It is the axe that fells the tree of illusion.

In terms of phenomena, our lives change, our bones and cells are transformed. But our true self is Buddha-nature, what in Christianity is called the Holy Spirit, and that never changes. It is not born and not destroyed. Through zazen we feel that the limited, relative ego is infinite, absolute existence. That is true satori. The practice of zazen itself becomes the real satori. Every zazen is a satori.

During zazen we can have the authentic experience of this satori, which is not a special or temporary state engendering other special states that are a product of personal, individual consciousness. The point is to have, through *hishiryo,* the physical experience of the sacred, universal consciousness. That does not come from the forebrain but from the hypothalamus and *kikai tandent* and that is why it is so important to concentrate on breathing out.

*Of the two main branches of Buddhism, Mahayana Buddhism is more concerned with saving and helping others than with personal salvation.
†The reservoir of the ocean of energy beneath the navel, which is filled and activated by your breathing in zazen.

THE EIGHT WAYS
TO WAKE UP
A GREAT PERSON

The zazen posture itself is God, Buddha.
It is the great person's satori.

1. *SHOYOKU* HAVE FEW DESIRES

Do not be ambitious, do not run after too many desires. Want little.

Buddha said, My dear disciples, you should understand that ambitious people, those who want only honors and profit, will suffer. People who have few wants, who limit their desires and do not have to be always running after things, looking for other objects, will not suffer so much.

We must practice *shoyoku*. That is the first way to wake up. Have few desires, or limit your desires.

In the end, that is the highest thing you can want.

2. *CHISOKU*   IT IS ENOUGH

When we receive something, it is enough. No desire is generated.

Buddha said, My dear disciples, if you wish to avoid much suffering, you must observe the Dharma of *chisoku,* it is enough. If you understand this, you can become truly rich, peaceful, calm, and free. People who understand and have woken up to this will feel at peace, will be free and joyful, even if they are sleeping on the hard ground. Those who do not understand *chisoku* and have not woken up to this will never be content, even if they sleep in great palaces. Whoever is not satisfied will always feel poor, even if he is rich.

3. *GYO*   QUIET, UNASSUMING JOY

Buddha said, My dear disciples, if you hope for true tranquility, true peace, true nirvana, satori, you must live away from the crowd and the street. You must live alone. Those who live quietly are respected by all the many gods of heaven.

But this does not only mean living physically alone; it is more a question of a state of mind. So, by being alone in the sense of being unattached, it is possible to extinguish the source of suffering.

4. *SHOJIN*   EFFORT

My dear disciples, said Buddha, strive unceasingly. Just as water flowing constantly over the same place can hollow out a rock, so it is necessary to continue. Trying to hurry, to force our way by willpower, only wears us out. Steadiness, habit are necessary. Repeating every day, not practicing in fits and starts, is important. Practice zazen every day.

Buddha said, My dear disciples, if you practice *shojin*— infinite, continuous, permanent effort—in striving for one thing, you will succeed in all things. So you must wake up to this and let your effort be uninterrupted.

5. *FUMONEN* NO ILLUSION

Protect the truth, the Dharma. Anything else is illusion. True meditation means returning to the normal, peaceful condition of body and mind, to *hishiryo* consciousness.

Buddha said, My dear disciples, if you want to find the true master, the true spiritual friend, do not mislead yourselves. Go straight on the way. Do not doubt. Those who realize *fumonen* are without illusion, and no thief can enter their houses. You must always control and regulate your mind, and see that your mind and consciousness are right. If you make a mistake, much merit will be lost. If the power of your consciousness is strong, you cannot be invaded by the five thieves: sex, overeating, love of honor, greed, and insanity.

Keeping to the right thought, not creating illusions, is like wearing armor. Non-illusion is the great satori, right consciousness, the great person's fifth way to wake up.

6. *SHU ZENJO* SAMADHI, THE PRACTICE OF ZAZEN

Shu = practice.
Zen = the Zen of zazen.
Jo = samadhi, stability, immobility.

Remaining in the Dharma, never *sanran,* never distracted: that is *zenjo.* Buddha said, My dear disciples, if you control your minds through zazen and samadhi, you can understand the cosmic order, the order of nature, the true aspect of exchange with the world, interdependence with the movement of the world.

Looking out, one sees many problems and senseless conflicts taking place all over the world. Many crises are occurring; and the most dangerous of all is within the minds of human beings. If we do not remain calm, things will grow more and more difficult. If we rediscover the normal condition, there will be no more need for conflict and rivalry, and the world will be peaceful. Please, keep trying always, practice zazen, and so you will achieve *jo*, stability, the condition of samadhi.

7. *JO RIKI*   THE ENERGY GENERATED BY ZAZEN

Jo = samadhi, the stability of zazen; *riki* = power, force. When you practice zazen, this power increases. In the modern world, most people have lost this power. It is not some sort of magic power; it is true, right energy.

8. *FUKERO*   NO ARGUMENT, NO RESISTANCE

What is *fukero?* Understanding and accepting the teaching of Buddha, letting go of one's own categories, one's own consciousness. Understanding the true aspect of the cosmos.

You must understand that your life and our world are only *mujo,* impermanent. That is the true aspect of life and the world. Do not suffer because of it, do not become sad. Make an effort, practice zazen, and wake up to the true satori that includes all of the great person's satoris.

✳ The light of true wisdom reveals much madness and darkness. Our life is dangerous, fragile; it cannot always be strong or go on indefinitely, becoming more and more glorious. Even if we grow rich and famous, even if we achieve political power or such fame that the whole world knows our names, it will not last forever, but will end like a burst bubble on the surface of the stream.

Zazen exactly includes these eight ways to wake up. Zazen includes everything. Through zazen you can experience the great person's ways to wake up.

What is satori? Without effort, simply throw away body and mind. Throw yourself away, go over to Buddha's side, follow the cosmic order. Then you act unselfconsciously, not by expending your own power or force. You can solve and stand away from the problems of life and death, and become Buddha himself.

HI SHI RYŌ

HISHIRYO

BEYOND THINKING AND
NOT-THINKING

The broad, deep sky is untroubled by the passing clouds.

What is *hishiryo?* Thinking without thoughts, not thinking but thinking. Beyond thought, it is absolute thought. You do not think, but your unconscious mind becomes active and you think unconsciously, with the thalamus, the central brain. What comes out is true thought, unthought thought, beyond thought.

It is impossible to cut off desires and illusions deliberately, it is not something we can will to happen. Little by little, however, in zazen, our desires cease to bother us; they diminish of themselves, unconsciously, naturally. We do not repress or pursue them —not push away, not run after—that is *hishiryo.*

There is no truth, no perfect reality; nor is there any real untruth or error. We must be beyond good and evil, beyond satori and illusion.

To experience satori, to wake up, means that the brain changes completely, comes back to its normal condition. Zazen is nothing other than the return to a normal condition. Satori is not some special state of the mind; the light of Buddha's third eye illuminates and overturns the whole world. Buddha experienced satori for all existences, all living beings, all the things in the universe.

> Just one voice . . .
> The moon at four in the morning,
> On the pillow; why can't people
> Wake up from their dreaming?

Suffering and illusions are the creations of our brain. We are constantly running after shadows, phantoms that we manufacture inside our own minds.

We must blot out the prints of illusions. It can be done by *hishiryo* consciousness. What *hishiryo* really means is to erase the traces left by foolish thoughts, to live without traces; that is true freedom. When you follow the cosmic system, it is no longer necessary to make categories.

We must think from the depths of unthinking. *Hishiryo* is the summit, the explosion, eruption, orgasm of consciousness, beyond thought; it is absolute, universal thought. *Hishiryo* is cosmic consciousness as distinct from individual consciousness; it is the ultimate consciousness, beyond space and time.

How do you think without thinking? That is the whole art of zazen. Concentrate on your posture and let your thoughts pass by, without dwelling at any point of consciousness: if you continue in this way during zazen, your thoughts become larger, they expand in length and depth until they reach the universal consciousness. We can get to this ultimate consciousness, but we cannot do it through the thoughts of our personal consciousness.

In regard to *hishiryo:* thought is thought but it is also not thought. Non-thought is non-thought but it is also thought.

76

In Zen we must neither reject nor select. If we do not chase after and we do not run away, then our mind is always serene. So it is said in the *Shodoka:* Do not grasp, do not turn aside.

Hishiryo cannot be expressed in words or defined by categories. It is the union of object and subject, objective and subjective. It is Zen. When we have returned to the state that precedes language and have a truly profound consciousness to express, then we can speak.

Then *hishiryo* becomes the source and root of creativity. It is the vast sky, king of samadhi, balance of the right and left hemispheres of the brain, control of self. Our personal minds limit the universal light, cosmic energy, the cosmic system; but *hishiryo* consciousness is totally merged with the cosmic system.

Shiki soku ze ku: Phenomena become emptiness.

Ku soku ze shiki: Emptiness becomes phenomena.

Shiki, existence, the world of phenomena, the visible, existential world in all directions, at all levels . . . is not distinguishable from *ku.*

During zazen, thoughts, the activity of both consciousness and the subconscious, gradually die away. We reach a state of harmony with the cosmic system, the original consciousness, the normal condition of the brain, not some special state of illumination.

Hishiryo is beyond all things, yet there is no notion of negativity involved. The substance of zazen is *hishiryo.* Phenomena, which are ever-changing, are governed by the law of impermanence. But the present instant is immutable. The substance of *shiki* is *ku.* The phenomenon of *ku* is *shiki.* We are born out of *ku.*

Behind the individual consciousness, ultimately, is absolute consciousness.

On the mirror-ocean, waves come and go. The tranquil surface wrinkles; then the waves fade, the surface of the sea is smooth again. *Hishiryo* is beyond our individual consciousness, beyond duality, and beyond the opposition of individual and *hishiryo* as well.

BO DAÏ SHIN

BODAI SHIN

THE RESOLVE
TO WAKE UP

What is waking up? Understanding the self. When you are awake you can stop trying, stop making vain efforts. Most people are forever searching this way and that, reading books, enrolling in complicated practices—but to no avail. It is possible to go straight, to go direct, by following the cosmic order. In our civilization today, every aspect of everyday life, of life in society, the economy—everything has turned us away from cosmic life. So sometimes we must return to the source.

If the working of our minds is wrong, then no good can come of any practice we try.

To wake up to the fundamental cosmic power is to wake up to yourself, to understand intimately your own profound nature.

The true, genuine Buddha-mind, the cosmic mind, is exactly like the moon, while the environment is like the surface of the water, or the current. Illusions are like the moon's reflection on the water.

All existences possess the truth and express the real state of universal truth.

Abandon, forget, let go of body and mind. *Shin jin datsu raku.* Only throw yourself into the house and family of Buddha, and Buddha will help, control, direct.

When you follow Buddha you do not need to use up your own strength, you do not need to make deliberate efforts with your own willpower. You can become Buddha unconsciously, naturally, automatically, detached from life and death.

Your posture, your zazen itself, is God or Buddha. There is no objective Buddha or God outside, on the other side. There is a subjective God or Buddha inside our mind, in ourselves. Our ego itself is the eternal God, Buddha. We are without birth and without death.

To practice zazen *mushotoku,* without any goal or desire for profit, is purity, strength.

Sometimes illusions rise up, but they pass away like dreams or clouds in front of the moon. Illusions are like the beggar who keeps hectoring you; you drive him off again and again but he keeps coming back, and then suddenly he gives up. You turn around to drive him off one more time, or give him some money to get rid of him, and there's nobody there. Satori.

Only grasp the original source, do not waste your time on the branches.

Through zazen, mental phenomena become like crystal; they reflect the moonlight.

Forget your personal body and mind; then there is room for absolute mind, non-ego. Harmonize, merge heaven and earth. The inner mind lets thoughts and emotions pass by, completely independent of its environment. The ego is abandoned.

That is the source of the philosophies and religions of Asia. Mind and body, outside and inside, substance and phenomena: these pairs are not dualities or opposed; they form a single, seamless whole.

When the mind's activity fills the cosmos, and we grasp opportunity as it arises, then we can arrange and cope with the ever-shifting flow of events, avoid accidents, tackle the ten thousand things in one. Original nature cannot be apprehended by our personal faculties and perceptions. What we grasp with our senses is not real, is not true substance, is imagination.

Difficult problems are different for each person, and we all need different means to solve them. We all have to create our own methods. We have to create by ourselves.

All great works of art go beyond technical mastery. Even in the fields of technology and science, the great discoveries come from somewhere beyond principles and techniques.

We must not be attached to just one idea, category, concept. From idea to act there must be freedom.

> *Not think:*
> *Was, will be;*
> *Behind, before;*
> *Only freedom*
> *At the middle point.*

What is *bodai shin?* The way. Not cogitate. Not seek. Not desire. Not keep. Not get. Not abandon.

As in the martial arts, ordinarily, technique must be acquired and used for the first ten or twenty years, but in the end what matters more is the state of mind. The link between mind and body, spirit and posture, attitude and technique, is breathing. In the end, posture and breathing become one.

The secret of the sword is never to draw the sword. Do not draw your sword, because if you try to kill someone else, then you will have to die yourself. What you need to kill is yourself, kill your own mind. If you have done that, other people will be afraid and run away. You will be the strongest and the others will keep their distance, and so it will not be necessary to fight or defeat them.

We must not think of winning, but we must not think of being defeated, either. That is contradictory; so what should we do? It is difficult; to lean left or right is easy, just as it is easy to win or lose. But not to win and not to be defeated, that is harder.

When our mind becomes egoless illumination, samadhi, then all desire and ambition disappear. There is nothing left. This is the last station in life, zero. We must come back to that point, that inner spirit; otherwise, our lives are full of trouble. Trying to obtain social status, or money, or a family, is not really necessary. Just be alone, face to face with yourself; you do not have to explain and show everything to others.

This is an inner, personal decision. Afterwards, life becomes as light as a passing cloud. If you follow Buddha with Buddha's energy and activity, there is no need to use your own energy or your own personal strength, or to disperse your consciousness, your mind. In the end we can become Buddha without separating ourselves from life and death. But we must not cling to or stagnate in any particular state of mind, or attach ourselves to anything that happens in the mind.

Samadhi is a delicate state, in which the body feels nothing except perfect peace in profound joy.

The spirit of samadhi is like the flame of a candle in a closed room; it breaks up the dark and throws light on all the objects around it.

The relationship between body and mind, physical and spiritual, self and society, self and all other existences, nature, cosmos, everything, is the same as that between the front and back of a single sheet of paper. Between the surfaces, there is nothing impure. Impurity is a demon. Originally, there is no demon between God or Buddha and the self; the two are completely intimate and united. But when an impure demon materializes, they become relative and dualistic. The demon of impurity creates disharmony between Buddha and the self.

We usually think of the things in nature—earth, streams, sun, moon, stars—as being outside our minds, but in reality they are the mind itself. Do not imagine, however, that this means that things exist only in our minds. Let go of the notions of outside and inside, going and coming. The individual mind is not outside, not inside. It goes and comes freely, without any attachment. A thought is mountain, water, earth. The next thought is a new mountain, new water, new earth. Each thought is independent, newly created, vital and instantaneous.

The undivided mind is not concerned with small and large, near and far, being or nonbeing, gain or loss, recognition or nonrecognition, satori or illusion, life or death. The undivided mind is beyond opposites. So the study of the mind is the way to achieve stable and undivided action, beyond all the worlds of relativity.

Our whole body-mind is *ku*, originally, and neither grows nor diminishes, neither is born nor dies.

Sometimes in our life and death, our desires for nirvana or other circumstances cause the Buddha-mind, the resolve to wake up, to develop in us. We should not wait for any particular time or place to realize that mind and resolve. It is never conditioned by time or space, any more than by intellectual capacity. Because the resolve to wake up is the origin of all true activity, it appears, naturally and automatically, of itself. It cannot be defined in terms of existence or nonexistence, good or evil, or circumstance, place, or past karma.

This life and this death are our true life, the life of every day with its suffering, sorrow, misfortune, difficulties, and also joy and good fortune. But the resolve to wake up arises more often in suffering and misfortune than in joy and luck. Happiness is like a bubble.

Beyond time and space there is neither existence nor nonexistence, nor good or bad persons or things. There is eternity. But in time, everything is *mujo*, ever-changing. To live eternally, we must understand the root, the source.

If you want to clean the river's mouth, you must go upstream first. To purify downstream, you must first purify the source.

LOVE, SUFFERING, FAITH, COMPASSION

Buddhism is neither ascetic nor hedonistic, neither self-denying nor self-indulgent, but between. The sexual energy in us can be used to reach a higher dimension of existence, to perform great deeds. When it is directed to a high dimension, then *shiki* becomes *ku*, phenomena are transformed into essence, and our sexual energy can accomplish great and holy things.

Why do human beings exist in this world? Because of karma. Karma does not know the fruit, the reward, and the reward does not know karma. In this place of not knowing is the true way.

The way is there and it does not linger, does not stop, it does not remain and does not go away, and it is not an impasse. The true inexhaustible treasure house lies within. This teaching is transmitted unconsciously, naturally, automatically, *mushotoku*. True pleasure comes unconsciously. A god who rules in the world of desires and tries to play upon desires becomes a devil.

It is not good to drink too much whiskey; but sometimes it is good to become a devil. It strengthens. Idealists can be deceived by illusions, morality is a cold thing, and asceticism can lead to madness. So the devil can be useful.

Both aspects exist together in our brains; sometimes we want to do evil and sometimes good. Our minds include both contradictory aspects, and it is impossible to cut them apart. In this respect, we are all alike.

What is perfect freedom? In itself, nothing is so very good, nothing is so very bad. If you choose materialism, you will be a victim of the present crisis of civilization. To play freely in the world, you must not pursue and not run away. If you have patience, you can become truly free.

Accepting without choosing is important. That has to do with faith. But blind faith is a mistake. If you have deep faith and your mind is *mushotoku*, however, great merits will appear, unconsciously, naturally, automatically. There is nothing to show or demonstrate: true faith is discreet—even, as far as possible, secret. God or Buddha exists in our minds. We must believe in ourselves. That is true faith.

During zazen, everybody becomes God or Buddha; there is no need to try to achieve that, or to be conscious of it; it's simply that the ego is connected to the total ego, the one that fills the whole cosmos. This body is the infinite cosmos. That is the only faith that can produce total effort without fatigue. The essence of faith is just that.

People suffer inside their illusions. The root of suffering is illusion. Illusion becomes suffering; we suffer from too many thoughts, too many worries, too much perplexity, depression, because we feel unloved, because we love too much, too intensely. We ache for somebody or something. The root of suffering is in our minds. The rich man suffers, the poor man suffers too. Fire is not only a material thing. The fire of the mind is more important. We must observe the fire of the mind. If we feel persecuted, who lights the fire?

Hell is not in some other world, it is in our minds. When

we look up, we see that we are alive, clinging to a vine that is being gnawed through by a black rat and a white rat.

If a thief enters a house to take money, or a gangster holds up a bank, he is never content with a part of the loot, half or ten percent; you have to give him everything. As long as there's anything left, he's not satisfied with a mere million or even five.

The egoist's mind, the mind of desire, is like the mind of the thief. Desire is born of jealousy, complexes. What is happiness? It has no form. We cannot decide anything about it or establish any category relating to it. Some people are always looking for happiness, but that is the same as looking for unhappiness. They are bound hand and foot.

All existences are bound together. They have the same root. You and I are tied together. Your happiness is my happiness. My happiness is your happiness. That is a true law or precept, having nothing to do with morality. If you understand the precept, you can understand morality. This isn't shallow moralizing, but true satori. The precept grows out of the spirit of compassion. Out of that precept is born the shower of pure nectar of the Dharma, the voice of the valley, beautiful music.

We must not lie to others or to ourselves. Lying to others is easy, but it is very hard to lie to oneself. We must not lie to others or to ourselves, and also we must not lie to the sky and the earth.

Our spirit of compassion grows through others; without others there can be no spirit of compassion or love. If we have patience, if we learn to face difficulties with patience, our capacity for patience increases. At the same time as our spirit of compassion develops, the strength of our faith grows alongside it.

The highest person understands everything in one decision. The person of ordinary dimensions hears much and cannot believe. If you accept people's criticism, those people become part of you; then the adversary vanishes and there's no longer someone criticizing. Life is often unfair. Is that bad? Too much heat or happiness causes our body and mind to melt, like sugar. Alone, we must be honest with ourselves, severe with ourselves; we must practice inside ourselves. That way, the person who criticizes us becomes our master, more truly than the person who admires us.

The bodhisattva lives in harmony with the world. If he wants to speak, he speaks. He doesn't need to say "do this or that"; he does not impose, he harmonizes, flexibly. But inside, there must be perseverence, steadiness; we must not let ourselves be pushed this way and that, and pretend that that is "harmony."

And we must not let ourselves be governed, ruled by either misery or joy. Just be tranquil and serene, as in zazen. The inner mind should be like that of a person inside a coffin. That is the normal condition, balance.

This has nothing to do with sacrifice. Abandoning the ego is not sacrifice. Abandoning the ego also means: receive everything. It is gain for the self and total gift for others. The two things remain inseparable.

To possess, to be attached: these are hindrances. One can fill an empty bottle, but nothing can be put into a bottle that is already full. If your mind is full of thoughts, if you are attached to your possessions, then wisdom cannot grow. A true life goes with other people.

Compassion without wisdom gives no real help, nor does wisdom without compassion. Sometimes we must hold hands with the devil, sometimes with pure beauty.

The right way is neither morality nor anti-morality. We must be flexible, sometimes dignified, sometimes easygoing; sometimes we need to be intimate, sometimes distant. If you want to become Buddha, you must be able to play every part, like a good actor; you must be able to assume every aspect. Too much attachment creates separation, in fact; it isn't real love, compassion. When we climb out of our fetters we can find true love, true compassion for Buddha, God, the dear family. Then your associates, your intimates will be truly happy.

Not run after . . . not run away.

In true religion there is no cruelty. The bodhisattvas of Mahayana Buddhism plunge into the filth and turpitude of human suffering. They do not choose whom they will help, they do not condemn or judge. They cannot rest so long as there is one more existence to be saved. How can you resist someone who has abandoned everything?

Give up gratitude, give up love, enter into nothing. Then you can become truly yourself, you can return, give back filial love, gratitude. Eternal love becomes possible. Real love is without attachment. If you can reach that, it is eternal love.

True religion means to seek the infinite, absolute way; and to seek the absolute, infinite, and eternal way, you must abandon body and mind.

In true love there is *shin,* faith. Holiness, faith, and compassion are not separate, they are one. When there is true love, there is faith in the other. If you are in doubt, you do not really love. In love, opposition is gone, dualism is gone; there is only unity, *hishiryo,* thinking without thinking. There is no opposition between thinking and not thinking. You are beyond thought. We have to embrace the viewpoint of the other person, understand that. If our thoughts are only a projection of our personal consciousness, we are constantly having to make choices.

The cosmic system includes everything. The sun shines for the whole universe; we must have universal compassion and a profound understanding of all things.

It is a truism that suffering is nourished, maintained, increased by mental rumination. Suffering is always the thought that one is suffering. And then one suffers even more. By letting one's thoughts pass by, in zazen, one can cut the roots of suffering. Empty the mind. Become like the man resting in his coffin. When one has learned this, things become relative again, as they should be.

In the face of death, nothing is so very important; most of the time, people suffer for things of little or no importance. During zazen the conditions in which the master teaches are a little like death, the moment of death, when many sufferings, especially moral ones, drop away. By means of the Zen education, you can unconsciously acquire the habit of assigning to moods, emotions, and perceptions their true value, which is often small. Why did Freud and all the psychoanalysts who came after him study the unconscious? Because the key to human fulfillment lies in eliminating or reducing the unconscious; it needs to be brought to the surface and dissolved, and so the artificial person is destroyed.

A very large part of suffering comes, of course, from the content of that unconscious over which people have no control, and that governs them without their knowledge.

Do not remain on the summit of the mountain of solitude.
Paddling muddy water by the landing-stage,
The highest spirit of compassion penetrates the three worlds.
You must be content to be a ferryman on the sea of sufferings.

TRUE FREEDOM

_____

The true wise man has no ego of his own; that way, all is ego.
True freedom, true wisdom, is like that.
If you possess some substance,
You can only possess some wisdom.

The very attitude of wanting to be free is a mistake. You must consider the law of interdependence; otherwise, if you make yourself into an autonomous entity with a will of its own, you will do nothing but lurch from one error to the next, colliding with the whole universe around you.

The highest way is not difficult; one has only to reject all discrimination.

We should not be influenced by either the admiration or the

disapproval of other people; non-attachment is the way to become free in this life.

Also, we should achieve the healthy desires we have; it is not necessary to eliminate them. How does one achieve such desires? Find desires of a high dimension to aspire to. That is the way to true freedom.

Please, try to let go. Let go once, just to see. Body and mind, what are they like? Their behavior, what is it like? Birth and death, what are they like? The law of Buddha, what is it like? The law of this world, what is it like? Mountains, rivers, the great earth, human beings, animals, houses, what are they like, when all is said and done?

If you consider these things up and down, inside and out, you will find, perfectly naturally, that the two particularized aspects of motion and stillness do not occur at all, and also that their non-occurrence is not at all the impassiveness of wood or stone. No one can fully comprehend such a thing; those who misunderstand are many. The person who studies the way by turning to Zen will obtain no illumination unless he knows that he himself is only halfway on the path. He must drop the mistaken notion that he has reached the end of the road. That is my prayer.

True freedom also means being satisfied with one's lot. One can always try to improve it, to go farther, to carry it beyond, higher. But not to complain, because that is just another self-indulgence, the same as being self-satisfied. Both are attachments, both lead to stagnation. The true attitude is to go freely forward, treating obstacles and delights alike as playthings.

Then all thoughts emanating from my mind and relating to myself must cease. Every day our lives give us an opportunity to deploy thoughts and reflections, but they often end in doubt. If we abandon all personal, dualistic thoughts, however, then self-evident, unhesitant thought arises, and is manifested as certainty.

There's no need to resist or run away from anything. And it's just as useless to run after anything.

91

Knowing the treasure of freedom does not mean intellectual knowledge, but knowledge of body and mind.

We have a body; but body is not self. We have a mind; but mind is not self. Self is nothing; it is interdependence with the environment, it has no permanent substance.

Truth and illusion, happiness and unhappiness, wealth and poverty, love and hate: it is impossible to adopt any criteria, because they differ for every human being. Everything is interdependence and so everything is *ku*, substanceless existence, without form and without definition.

In our everyday life, people reflect one another. If you are angry, the person across from you becomes angry too; it's like a reflection in a mirror. If you smile, the other person smiles too, because all the phenomena in the universe have the same root. If our minds are pure, everything around us—trees, wind, birds, everything—becomes pure. If one single person practices zazen, that person influences the whole cosmos; the whole cosmos reflects that zazen.

A mirror reflects a form, any and every form. If you smile into the mirror, the mirror smiles back at you. The mirror is *ku*, like our minds during zazen. During zazen we can see ourselves more clearly, as in a mirror. Our unconscious is reflected in our minds. The seeds of karma in our unconscious are manifested. But the object of the mirror's reflecting our unconscious is not to judge that this is good and that is bad. The mirror's reflection is truly objective.

Life is becoming more and more difficult nowadays. If we are to escape a catastrophe, we must develop the potential for human activity in the future, transform people's minds and consciousness, recover the power of spiritual freedom.

Wanting to keep and possess things, like wanting to abandon them, is a cause of painful contradictions; and so we invent lies, embellishments, imitation. The mind that chooses is not authentic, but an imitation. Categories and concepts, lines of reasoning, may seem beautiful and brilliant to commonplace minds. But in comparison with the cosmic order they are not so very beautiful or intelligent, or true.

Some people try to practice in such a categorizing state of mind, but they can't do it because they are always trying to find out *why*. They become complicated, and in the end they mistake their own son for the enemy.*

Wanting to abandon illusions and seize hold of the truth is also an illusion. In other words, we should not create either illusions or truth in our own minds and by our own will. To say that poverty is misery and wealth happiness is a mistake. For a newborn child, neither one exists or has meaning. A baby has no illusions and knows no God or ghosts or hell. Later, people teach it the names of categories and mental illusions, and its pure spirit is damaged, destroyed.

Once one has passed through the gateway of Zen, the whole closed system of illusion that is the human consciousness dissolves. True wisdom has no boundaries. Sometimes the people who criticize us can be our good masters. We must take each thing as medicine for the happiness of life.

Since anything can be the way, can bring happiness, nobody can know what really corresponds to good or evil. The heavens themselves cannot predict whether events will signify progress or regression.

Zazen, the return to oneself and one's sources by means of silent sitting, helps to eliminate karma. In a real religion, free will means something; one should be able to change one's destiny. We must not let ourselves be influenced by other people; what we have to do is understand our true nature so that we can discover the sense and truth of our activity in the world.

A friend tells you to look at the beautiful moon. But all you look at is the friend's finger pointing at the moon, and you wonder what the moon itself can be like. You look for the truth in the finger, and so you continue to be mistaken.

A person who knows true freedom cannot be attacked by

*An allusion to a famous Zen anecdote.

93

anyone or disturbed or influenced by anything, because that person is following the cosmic force, like a great elephant that does not try to play on the rabbits' path. That person's thoughts are above those of ordinary people.

Ordinary people cannot disrupt the cosmic order, although they are always trying. All they do, though, is wear out their strength, their personal strength. The cosmic power protects the person of satori.

MASTER-DISCIPLE

Dear friend, don't you see:
The man of satori
Has closed his book
And is still.
He does not try to push away illusion.
He does not try to ferret out the truth.

A master does not have to be old, his age is unimportant; all that matters is that he has understood the true law and has himself been certified by a true master. In him, written words are not important, nor is understanding; he must have enormous energy and boundless will. The person who is not attached to individual views and does not stop at surface knowledge, the person whose actions and understanding correspond exactly, is a true master.

Once you have met a true master you must drop all your old relationships.

When Eka* met his true master, he cut off his arm: you must feel, understand by yourself. And when you have decided, you must continue forever. That is the meaning of Eka cutting off his arm. You must abandon, be resolute. Do not waste time. Continue your effort, practice zazen and *sampai*† with the master. Do not argue, do not lose your temper, just continue practicing *gyoji* (persevering spiritual practice) and *dokan* (the ring, daily cycle of the way). Your mind must be non-mind, nothing in it, even if you have doubts. That way, you will not suffer from the demon of other people's criticism and the folly of fools. Sometimes friends influence for the worse and pull us into the wrong way. Stupid friends become demons.

It is hard to continue. Sometimes one loses patience and wants to run away. But even if the master is angry you must perform *sampai* and continue. That is *raihai toku zui*, obtaining the master's marrow. *Raihai* means to lay your body on the ground, to reach the marrow by throwing yourself down in *sampai*.

In Zen, there is zazen and also *raihai*. *Raihai* is the action of the body, performed sincerely, without affectation or formalism.

Raihai is not bowing down before God. It is becoming one with the divine, the human particularity becoming *ku*. Your body and those of others forming one.

My master, Kodo Sawaki, always used to say, "Shave your head, put on the *kesa*, and practice zazen: that is the highest happiness in life."

Before anything else, the *kesa* is the symbol of simplicity; it is eternal life, infinite light, the true symbol of universal love.

*Eka was the second Chinese patriarch; his master was Bodhidharma, first Chinese patriarch and twenty-eighth in line from the Buddha.

†*Sampai* is a triple prostration performed by master and disciples together, for the purpose, among other things, of showing mutual respect.

What is the transmitted *kesa?* From patriarch to patriarch it has been transmitted; from master to disciple without interruption, even for one generation. It is the thread of Zen. It is not just a piece of cloth. The *kesa* itself is zazen, and vice versa. Zazen and *kesa* are one. *Kesa* and zazen are like the two wings of a bird.

Even very sincere people who practice zazen for a long time cannot do so much to change their karma as long as they do not put on a *kesa.* But if they wear it, their ego disappears and then, unconsciously, naturally, automatically, the mind becomes gentler, softer.

If we put on the *kesa,* unconsciously, naturally, automatically, our mind is invested with great compassion. Putting on the *kesa* means winning the highest victory. One's life becomes nobler than that of any minister, king, or emperor.

You do not put on the *kesa* for your own self only. It influences other people, who can find true happiness through your *kesa;* it can lessen the sufferings of other people. But above all, the *kesa* should be a symbol of simplicity, of all that is most poor and bare; it is a humble garment, without decoration.

The *kesa* is not a quantity or a quality. It has a color, but it is not a color that you can name. It has no limit. Its color is not red or white or black or blue. It is always dark, but beyond definition.

The *kesa* is so vast that it becomes infinite, formless; yet its form must be exactly as it is.

In itself, the *kesa* is not a material thing. It is the symbol of life, cosmic truth.

When one practices the supreme, perfect satori, it is very hard to be taught by a true good master. A true master can be a man or a woman; but the master must be a great person, better than a hero. The master must be a satori person, not a person of the past or the present—beyond time, both old time and new.

That is the true fundamental aspect of the true master who gives his or her marrow.

Only such persons can transmit goodness and never be governed by any thought originating either in their own minds or in those of others.

Once you have met your true master, you must concentrate on practicing the way, making an effort, by means of thought and non-thought, by means of all your mind and half your mind. You must practice as though your hair were on fire.

If you practice like that, you can never be troubled by friends who mislead and criticize you. The story of the patriarch who cut off his arm and obtained the master's marrow is not the story of any person other than yourself. You are already the master who has shed body and mind.

Intellectual learning stifles. One must get rid of it or go beyond it, learn to use it in moderation and keep the mind open. The wisdom that is learned must work hand in hand with intuitive wisdom, and the latter can appear only when the mind is freed.

Obtaining the master's marrow, or the transmission of the true Dharma, is accomplished by sincerity and faith. Sincerity and faith come neither from outside nor from within.

The Dharma is far more important than your little body.

It is not possible for you to transmit your body. If we attach the slightest importance to our body and make light of the Dharma, the Dharma cannot be transmitted or the true way attained. Give all your weight to the Dharma, lighten your own body, and, please, as much as possible, withdraw from the affairs of the world and make your home in the way.

What is the use of the samurai's attitude, his powerful will? It is to lighten his own body and lean upon the Dharma. Many methods exist, but one must practice on one's own initiative, without depending on any other teaching. You must esteem the Dharma more than any other thing. If a stone, a pillar, a wild fox were to possess the true Dharma and obtain the master's marrow, then you must make every effort, sacrificing even your body and mind, to serve them. If you do not practice like that, it is very hard to find the true Dharma.

A great master is a great servant;
Always he must be thinking of his disciples.

Each person must be taught differently. The point is to seize the right opportunity, the appropriate chance, that will give each person true faith and strengthen the source of the spirit.

Teaching consists in leading the disciple to the river's edge. Where is the stream filled with pure water to drink? The cow does not know, so the farmer must lead her there. Through their zazen, teaching, lectures, the masters are simply walking alongside their disciples. Over and over again: repetition is very important in teaching. It is hard to be awake . . . but continue, repeat. After a while, the cow learns the way to the river's edge and can go by herself.

Please, wake up sober from the intoxication of the illusions and sins and drunkenness of this world, and join the vast cosmic community. The community must help all sentient beings, because every one of them must be saved. That is the meaning of a true *sangha* (community) and a true *sesshin* (period of intensive practice).

But you must not be intoxicated by religion, either. Beware of religion. In Mahayana Buddhism we learn to wake up sober. You should not be intoxicated, or ecstatic, or esoteric.

Some people cultivate a state of ecstasy during zazen. They are wrong. A truly religious person must not sell esoteric liquor to believers, or ecstatic liquor or mystical liquor.

The master understands everything, but he must look at the disciple's mind. If the disciple has faith, the line of separation, duality, difference, and opposition melts into unity, unity between master and disciple, without any opposition.

The master is the master.
The disciple is the disciple.
But the master is also disciple.
The disciple is also master.

If the master is shaken by the disciple's words, he cannot understand the disciple's will and consciousness. If the master is in disharmony with words, he is in danger of falling into doubt.

But if the disciples are shaken by the master's words, they will stumble into the abyss, and disagreement will lead them too into the dead-end of doubt.

Sometimes, teaching must be strong. Compassion is not only gentleness. A sharp blow of the *kyosaku,* the stick of awakening, placed just right, is also an act of compassion.

HERE AND NOW

———

All you who seek the way,
Please,
Do not waste this moment now.

Watch out, watch out! I hear you repeating these words over and over again, but I want to tell you: Do not use this language to other people; please, address it to yourself.

Give all your attention, your watching out, to your own way; do not imitate other people. Your life is unique and your karma your own. Do not even try to imitate Buddha or Christ; follow their teaching, understand the essence, the depth and reach of it, and create your own way in relation to your own life.

Our life:
To what can it be compared?
The dewdrop shaken from the heron's bill
That reflects the full light of the moon.

When we meditate on impermanence, thoughts of *me* and *mine* do not arise, any more than thoughts of fame and interest.

Impermanence cannot be apprehended by cerebration. Everything is in constant flux.

Even if the body dies, the spirit becomes one with the cosmic power and lives forever. You must have that conviction.

If you have that conviction very strongly, then you can become more and more happy, you can live for eternity in this life, starting now, not only after you die. Here and now, your life becomes eternity.

If I must die here and now, what will be the state of my spirit, my mind? If I must die next week, or next month, shall I go on mumbling and rehearsing the trivia of my self? We must not forget that death can come at any moment. Then we can sense the flight of time and not waste our lives. Then we can make every instant full, do what it is important to do now, and not put off anything until tomorrow. Here and now must be complete, finished. Then there will be no time in which to regret time's passing. We should be frightened by the flight of time. For a great many people, life happens in the future. They are always putting things off until later, they spend the present thinking about the future.

And time passes, years go by, a life ends, it is too late, the time has come to die. A dream. Life passes like a dream, skimming past. I'm sixty years old now, perhaps I shall live another ten or twenty, maybe even thirty years. It's very short, the length of a dream.

If you are totally present to yourself, concentrating in body and mind, in the fullness of here and now, without holding anything back, an instant can become eternity. This instant now is all that is important, it is eternity; past and future are nothing but dreams and imaginings, visions.

All time, all life is only an instant, and so it is impossible to analyze, categorize, conceptualize. It is only a series of steps, so many here-and-nows. So the most precious thing in our life is to walk along the path, the way that has never been tried, that is never experienced twice.

Time is not a line, but a series of now-points.

How should we be? How should we act? How should we behave here and now? That is the koan, the life-and-death problem, of Zen.

Through zazen, eliminating our bodies and minds and those of all other existences, we can go beyond everything, beyond the beyond. In one instant.

And in the end we must not cling and dawdle, even in the tracks of satori. We must realize the cosmic system at the point now. The One is in that point, which is beyond everything.

Experience is here and now. Time exists only now, existence exists only now. The past and future are not existence. Every instant experienced is a point, and the series of points makes a line but leaves no trace. Only here-and-now exists.

It is completely senseless to think about what comes after death, about heaven, paradise. It is not necessary to ask questions about what we become after this life. Such questions are the fruit of egoism, and torment people unnecessarily.

Here-and-now contains eternity.

To practice zazen here and now is to practice the true teaching of Buddha. There are no degrees or steps, zazen itself is satori, here and now we are Buddha.

If human beings did not exist, there would be no need for God or Buddha, so we must not look for the meaning of those concepts in some other place. They exist here and now, in our body and in our mind.

When the fish swims in water
There is no end to the water.

103

When the bird flies through the sky
There is no end to the sky,
However far it flies, however near.

But if, after swimming through the water, the fish wants to go farther; and if, after flying through the sky, the bird wants to find a larger space, they cannot find any path or fixed point in the water or the sky.

If you discover this place, your behavior will be right and you will find your way naturally. If you find this path, your behavior will be the realization of truth in everyday life. This path and place cannot be grasped by such relative concepts as *large* and *small* or *self* and *others*, just as they are neither present since the beginning nor do they emerge suddenly now. They are there, just as they ought to be.

Here and now: space is most important, but here is less important than now. Time is not a line. Now never comes back. We can come back to here but never to now. Now is the present tense of the cosmos, perpetually changing.

MŪ JŌ

MUJO

IMPERMANENCE

We all have a body that is holy and splendid.

Now we must follow the way of *mujo,* impermanence, the eternal changing of all things.

What shall we do, for our body, our life?

Everything is *mujo,* impermanent, for every one of us. We are like dreams, a soap bubble, a dewdrop, an image. Our life and our body are like that.

Of all the things that live, ruled by the antagonistic and complementary effects of the two poles *yin* and *yang* in every point of space between heaven and earth, there is not one that escapes change and death. The dreadful and awesome demon of *mujo* never stops spying on your for one instant, and attacks suddenly, before you realize what is happening. All phenomenal existences are as ephemeral as a falling star, a dream, a bubble in the current of the stream, a shadow, a drop of dew on the grass at dawn, a bolt of lightning, a floating cloud.

If a person in a boat looks at the shore, he may mistakenly imagine that it is the shore that moves; but if his gaze is fixed intimately on the craft itself, he will understand that in reality it is the boat that is moving. In the same way, if we try to understand the nature of phenomena using nothing more than our own muddled personal perceptions, we make the mistake of imagining that permanence is an attribute of our nature.

We must understand that our ego is as impermanent as everything else in this fleeting world.

A moment does not come back; it exists only that moment. Dogen wrote, "Time is neither good nor bad, but good and bad are time. Time does not choose between good and evil, but good and evil choose time."

Our experience of everyday life takes place in time and space. We cannot go beyond those two parameters or have any experience outside them.

Our life and world are constantly changing, constantly all things are vanishing, throughout the world of phenomena conditioned by time and space. There is no eternal or permanent substance. In Mahayana Buddhism, neither person nor existence has substance. All existences are substanceless and governed only by relationships of interdependence.

The true wise man has no ego, no particularity, whereas madmen and fools have powerful egos that they are unable either to govern or abandon.

Everybody has two aspects, front and back, outside and inside. Even people who are a long way away can return to a normal condition one day. Many phenomena arise in our lives; good becomes evil, and sometimes order is changed into disorder. We have to face things: yet when we face physical or other difficulties, sometimes we lose sight of the truth, reality.

As we live on, unhappiness and problems mean happiness, just as the leaves that die in autumn mean spring. Outside our minds, there is no happiness or unhappiness; only our minds decide. We may be poor, have nothing, and also find true happiness.

All existences, all phenomena, are like a dream. They are like a shadow, a drop of water, a bolt of lightning. Everything changes and never stops.

LIFE
AND DEATH

Like a dream, a phantom, or a flower of emptiness, that is our life. Why should we suffer by trying to seize this illusion?

Death also is a dream.

Life is a dream. Life and death are the same. Life and death, the point in time. The point is only a point, it does not continue, but looked at as an object, the point becomes a line. In reality, there is no trace. Life is just one point. Death is just one point. Time must not use us, we must use time. Living is like the current of fresh water in the stream. The current stops and we are in the presence of death.

Zazen is observing death while we are alive. Only the people who solve the problem of death, their own death, can find true happiness in life. Through zazen we can be inside our coffin alive, and, naturally, automatically, unconsciously, find a solution to the problem of death. There is no need to fear death. Dying is the natural continuation of life. Life is a phenomenon, a mushroom on the earth. We are eternally being born. What we call life and death do not exist; they are not separate. In death, activity ceases but the body, being transformed, returns to the cosmos. Even if it is cremated or thrown into the sea, the component elements of the body are still there one hundred or six hundred years later. When we think that our body will be changed into a handful of dust, we should not feel sorry to lose body and life. Fear neither life nor death.

The phenomenon of our body is just one of our sorrows.

The dead cannot go backward or forward. We live, so we shall have to experience death. But if we live, we should become as the dead, and wake up. The dead do not need to wake up.

What happens to the soul after death? Reincarnation, transmigration can be neither affirmed nor denied. In Buddhism you'll find little commentary on metaphysical questions; they're not considered important. If you are too preoccupied by them, you think too much and lose energy. This is not a religious problem. Philosophies are games played with ideas: Is there immortality of the soul? Or, Is death the end of everything? Or, Life is only once; well, then, let us make the most of it.

Buddhism talks about existence only in the form of phenomena. It has nothing to say about substance. Its comments on life relate to visible things and experiences. It is impossible to debate questions of metaphysics; there is no way our form of knowledge can decide them.

If we understand that there is no substance to the ego, then we are connected to the cosmos and all existences. There is no more self or others as distinct entities, but only interdependence. That is letting go of the ego.

The harder we try to stop our illusions, the more they grow. Some people look at the person in front of them and their minds start humming away; or they order themselves to stop thinking deliberately. But during zazen what we must do is look inside ourselves. Our illusions appear. We can observe them objectively. Zazen itself becomes the mirror.

> The Buddha way transcends relative and absolute,
> And so, birth and death exist.
> Existence and satori exist.
> Even so, the flowers, although we love them,
> Fade and die;
> And even so, the weeds, although we hate them,
> Grow and thrive.

Even if we love the flowers, they wilt; even if we hate the weeds, they grow. Do not make the mistake of adoring heaven, paradise. Do not fear hell after death. Hold out your hand and stretch your body beyond the three worlds. Follow the cosmic order always, and attach yourself to nothing.

When we forget ourselves completely, profoundly, intimately, our body-mind becomes one with the whole cosmos. That is satori. There is no more inside or outside, subjective or objective or dualism or relativity. If we forget everything, then everything is resolved in the instant. Here-and-now is a point; if we concentrate on that point, point by point we shall make a line and can come to our death without needing to feel anxious.

Our life is suffering, it is full of difficulties and complications; but during zazen it is possible to realize that this kind of suffering is foolish; it is possible to observe ourselves, see and understand ourselves, and cut off the cause of suffering; to transform ourselves into truly liberated, peaceful persons, without attachments and without fear. Thinking, on the other hand, mulling over and over, feeding thoughts, only creates more suffering. We must let everything pass, pass, pass, not stagnate, not dwell upon any one thought. The habit acquired during zazen rubs off on everyday life, and life becomes peaceful and simple. True wisdom can arise. Through zazen we can understand our own nonsubstantiality, and through the wisdom that then arises we can become like the dragon slipping into the water or the tiger entering the mountain.

You can become completely free; that is, you can rid yourself of all contingencies and act beyond them, independently of their substance, nature, and force.

When wood has turned to ashes it cannot turn back to wood; but we are not to think that the ashes are after and the wood before. We must understand that wood remains in its dharmic position as wood and that it has a before and an after. However, although there is a before and an after, the before and after are sharply distinct. Ashes too remain in their dharmic position as ashes, and also have a before and an after.

Life is one potential position and death is another potential position. It is like the relationship between winter and spring: it is not right to say that winter is transformed into spring, or that spring becomes summer.

ESSENCE AND PHENOMENA INTERMINGLE

———

The cosmos is movement and not-movement.
Movement is born of not-movement,
The two give rise to each other.
The planet's revolution is born of the
Immobility of the skies.
The eternal skies are born of light.
Light,
Source of the cosmic order.

KAKU NEN MU SHŌ

KAKUNEN
MUSHO

UNFATHOMABLE EMPTINESS,
NOTHING SACRED

The fundamental root of Buddhism is *kakunen musho*.

Kakunen: the infinite, open sky.

Musho: not sacred or holy.

There is no such thing as holiness or as foolishness. That is the essence of Zen. During zazen it is not necessary to think about becoming a saint, God or Buddha. Not necessary to do anything. Be beyond time and space, all through the cosmos. When Dogen speaks of north, south, east, or west he is not talking only about the cardinal points. True religion always embraces contradictions. Zen is beyond categories.

"What is the most holy truth?" asked the emperor Liang.

"Kakunen musho," said Bodhidharma.

Kakunen = empty; *musho* = beyond saintliness. Complete emptiness, where there is no more anything, beyond holiness or sacrilege. In *kakunen musho* there is no floor or ceiling or floorboard or roof. No beneath, no above, no wind, no south gate, east gate, west gate, north gate. No rug, no floor, no pillar. There is neither good nor evil, neither hatred nor love. There is the pure sky, cloudless, blue, immense, infinite. There is no point of contact, everything is infinite. That is *kakunen musho.* Beyond sanctity and sacrilege.

Beyond the mountain, beyond good and evil, beyond life, beyond satori, illusions, everything. Beyond right, left, Christianity, Buddhism. In this manner you can reach the ultimate truth, which is beyond all attachment. To negotiate the way, you must efface, cut all traces.

Be beyond Buddha, the demon of holiness.

In Mahayana Buddhism, understanding does not come at the end of some meticulous analytical process; it is a synthetic, intuitive, direct vision of *ku.* That is the point of departure of all understanding. Starting from the intuition of *ku,* all phenomena can be understood. All existences are in flux; all are condemned to life and death. All sentient beings and all inanimate objects are governed by the same universal law: birth, development or growth, decay, and death or extinction.

Our birth moves inexorably toward our death. Why be afraid of it? Why refuse it?

One can die anytime, here and now. Nothing is more natural. We cannot decide how long our life will last or when we shall die.

The body changes, develops, is transformed, and so it is with the mind. There is no lasting substance, no entity to our ego.

The law of interdependence maintains all the relationships and interactions of the realm of phenomena in a perfect state of balance; water and air, the human body and the galaxies, all are governed by this law in the perfect harmony of interrelationships.

Phenomena are the direct result of karma, which means action, motion. Motion, movement comes from *ku,* is the phenomenal aspect of *ku;* so all phenomena are shadows of *ku,* shadows of the original spirit. *Ku* transcends the extremes, the polarities. It is the middle way of Buddhism, that lies beyond all opposites.

Our world of phenomena is a dualistic world, which starts in *ku* and culminates in *ku*. Understanding this law, not with the intellect but through the experience of realization in the body, is satori. It can be understood unconsciously, naturally, automatically, in zazen.

Shiki corresponds to the provisional, temporary, momentary, ephemeral aspects or structures. *Shiki* is the constantly moving structure of manifested cosmic power. *Ku* is the non-manifested cosmic potential, infinite and eternal because it is present in the infinity of things and immutable in its nature. It is both transcendent and immanent.

Each thing is created, composed, assembled by a chain of causes and interdependences. Every material phenomenon is *shiki* and has no substance, does not exist in isolation.

In the beginning, all is *ku*, all existences are *ku*. All existences are manifestations of the law of interdependence.

What is the essence of life? Self? Consciousness? Mind? Where do you situate substance?

KU

VACUITY

Ku is empty, but that is not all it means. Sometimes it should be translated "the totality of the cosmos." The ideogram can mean either the void or the sky. It is also the circle that includes everything.

The true nature of *ku* is neither existence nor nonexistence, but both at once, depending on one's viewpoint.

All things are change. Out of *ku*, emptiness, phenomena are born; and in the end everything returns to *ku*, zero. All things start from zero and come back to zero, including the cells of our body.

The Hannya Shingyo Sutra says that in the realm of *ku*, of vacuity, nothing grows and nothing decreases. In *ku*, everything equals zero. It is *mu shin*, no mind, no consciousness.

During zazen your mind moves from thought to thought or from non-thought to thought, or from thought to non-thought or from non-thought to non-thought. In any case, the point of intersection is zero. Whenever your state of consciousness moves, changes, you pass through zero.

Ku is the Japanese word for the Sanskrit term *sunyata,* the void, relativity. This is not a negation of existence per se, but an affirmation of the relativity of existence, which is dependent upon causality and the interdependence of all other existences.

The factors of causality are changing all the time; there cannot be such a thing as a static existence. So *sunyata* denies the possibility of any form of static phenomenal existence; all phenomena are relative and depend upon other phenomena.

Everything, even the law or Dharma, is *sunyata,* relative, and hence dependent. Thus, *sunyata* must not be confused with the negation of the existence of phenomena in any form. *Sunyata* is the cosmos, existence without substance, the principle of *ku.*

During zazen we experience deep tranquility. The brain grows calm. We can meditate profoundly. Many ideas arise.

If you want true wisdom you must continue zazen; and after zazen, through zazen, true wisdom can develop; because all phenomena are created out of *ku.*

But neglecting existence for the sake of *ku* is also a sickness, like diving into water in order to get away from the rain or plunging into fire to escape from fire. That is stagnant zazen, and it is the product of a deluded effort to grasp the truth. That kind of zazen becomes decoration, artifice; it is sheer technique, imitation.

If you are merely applying a method, you will become weak or stupid. If you don't understand, then practice, do nothing but practice. That way, if you make a mistake, it will be only a phenomenon, *shiki.*

All existences, all illusions, are ultimately *ku.* And in reality there is neither illusion nor disillusion, neither true nor false, neither darkness nor light. Total light is all darkness and all darkness becomes light.

Light is the world of differentiation; in darkness identity

reigns. Light becomes dark, dark becomes light. Buddha-nature becomes human existence, and so human existences are Buddha-nature, original nature.

At death, body and consciousness disappear while karma and cosmic life continue eternally; to die means to go back to *ku*, our true essence.

According to the Buddhist philosophy of *ku*, all the existences in the cosmos, or the reality of all phenomena, must be denied; and even in ourselves there is no fixed or immovable central substance.

Originally, the Buddha way transcends itself, and there is no notion of abundance or lack. Nevertheless, there are appearance and disappearance, illusion and satori, sentient beings and Buddha. But even though that is so, the flowers fade, however much we love and miss them, and weeds grow, however much we neglect and spurn them.

When we look at life full on, there are two contradictory things: difference and identity, affirmation and negation. How can we find or create the real value of our life?

To apprehend all phenomena, all existences, as the truth that engenders activity and creates—this is creative logic, beyond the affirmation of phenomena and the negation of phenomena. So what can solve the inner problems of the mind is the possibility of following, of applying this logic. It embraces all the contradictions in the world, without drawing a line between object and subject.

Nothing is not opposed to existence; it is true freedom—always stable, fearless, unimpeded. Illumination without any impediment in all directions. The eternal fundamental energy that fills the cosmos. It is God, Buddha, more.

Our body is always matter and mind in interdependence. So *atman*, the absolute, exists here and now, but at every instant it changes, like the cells in our bodies.

There is no substance to the self. Body and mind and all the existences of the cosmos are changing endlessly.

SHIKI SOKU ZE KU

KU SOKU ZE SHIKI, SHIKI SOKU ZE KU

VACUITY BECOMES PHENOMENA, PHENOMENA BECOME VACUITY

Ku soku ze shiki, shiki soku ze ku. We must go beyond, transcend both *shiki* and *ku.*

We have to be beyond difference and sameness. We have to be beyond *shiki* and *ku,* beyond thought and non-thought. Then we reach *hishiryo* consciousness.

The law governing the manifestation of the fundamental cosmic power is interaction; in other words, when the cosmic potential manifests itself, it disperses and gives material form to cosmic energy, which divides and organizes itself according to the law of interdependence. It is this law alone that gives matter its appearance as phenomena.

> *If you look at* ku, *see also* shiki.
> Ku soku ze shiki.
> *If you see* shiki, *look also at* ku.

Shiki soku ze ku.
Ku *is transformed into* shiki, shiki *into* ku.

The whole of the Hannya Shingyo Sutra, the Sutra of Great Wisdom, revolves around this formula.

If you understand this relationship, everything becomes easy. You do not have to think about it with your brain but realize it fully through your body. Start from the phenomena—*shiki*—of our everyday life and return to *ku*—zazen. And from *ku* return to *shiki,* to help all sentient beings and harmonize with them.

If you concentrate on zazen for an hour or two every day, then you can plunge into phenomena, merge with the cosmic ego, and spread wisdom in your everyday life. Then zazen becomes the helm, the steering wheel of every movement of your life.

True concentration is not thinking or non-thinking, it is beyond thought: it is absolute thought. It is a return to the original *ku,* arising out of concentration.

Potentially, concentration in *ku* contains expansion into *shiki.* Potentially, expansion into phenomena, *shiki,* contains the return to concentration in *ku.*

We find in *ku* the infinite and eternal; so *ku* is a synonym for nirvana, and in fact it is nothing other than the middle way.

Mujo is change, the unborn, without beginning or end. No birth, no death, only change. There is no beginning or end of the cosmos. You can see bubbles in the current of a stream; first, water turns into a bubble, then the bubble turns back into water.

When we die, our life does not end. We return to the cosmos like the bubbles that burst on the surface of the stream.

We must understand what lives eternally, what does not.

Often, people love purity and hate impurity. Originally, however, all phenomena, all the existences in the cosmos, are neither pure nor impure. Everything is identical. But by virtue of our thoughts and actions we create separations, particles, mud. On this planet the earth, mountains, rivers, forests, and oceans are not impure, not pure. That is nature.

Purification, the pure land, is not in some other country or after death. Here and now the pure land must be built.

If your mind, your consciousness, is set right; if your speech and behavior are right; if the three attitudes of mouth, body, and consciousness are right, then the environment becomes right.

Through perception, consciousness, and sensations, things change, now pure, now impure, and desires are born. . . .

Purity, impurity: it is impossible to decide. Our real personality, our original spirit is without purity or impurity, just as the cosmos is.

At birth, the consciousness of the baby has no impurities at all. A newly conceived baby has nothing to do with purity or impurity. Then, little by little, it is influenced by karma—its heredity from its parents, the environment, the people around it, its education, which nowadays is often distorted and distorting. Karma knows nothing about compassion, result, effect, and vice versa. Where is fault? Merit? Only the consciousness of human beings makes distinctions about such notions.

There is no duality. No beginning or end. No impurity or purity. No increase or decrease. This can be illustrated by the metaphor of water and waves. This morning there is a storm and, no doubt, huge waves at sea. When the storm clears the waves subside, but the water in the ocean is neither more nor less than before the storm.

Impermanence: the perpetual changing of all things—in other words, nonentity, existence without any substance. The instant it is born, the flame dies; the flame burning in this instant has nothing to do with that of an instant ago. Flame is a living representation of nonsubstantiality.

A potential is the only permanent component of each form of the manifest, which is itself impermanent and a product of impermanence. A potential is permanent because it is for all eternity in everything that is and everything that is not. It is independent, because it is the cause and condition of everything that exists. It is the motor that causes what has been manifested to move. A potential exists in every force-form and in all the relationships connecting force-forms, from the infinitely small to the infinitely great.

Within every manifestation is the plenitude of potentiality, which itself contains the totality of manifestation. This potentiality is the fundamental cosmic power, *ku,* nothing, the non-manifest, and it is also the great All and the manifest, in that which the All and manifest have, in their evolution and change, of non-manifest and potential—just as a seed is the non-manifested tree and contains all the potentiality of the tree.

In any event, all existences are simply *ku,* without substance. Everything exists without existing, everything exists only in change and through change, and what subtends change is potential. We must understand that *mujo,* change, is eternity.

In Zen there is no separation between material and spiritual; all impressions are spiritual, but are also recorded in the neurons of the brain in the form of information that is capable of actualization at any moment.

Seeds of karma that have been deposited live on after death and must of necessity manifest themselves, according to the universal law that says that any seed must either germinate or perish (be transformed) in due course. The seeds will become the heredity of a newborn child, investing it at ovulation; its potential is contained in the sperm of the father and ovum of the mother.

If a seed does not germinate, it must be transformed. That is what happens during zazen. Bad karma appears, freeing itself from the unconscious. But through the action of zazen in the consciousness, freed from perception and the ignorance that is its consequence, our bad karma can come to an end—that is, can be transmuted and regenerated in the original pure consciousness.

Then, emptied of the seeds of karma, the mind opens to the eternal and immutable, merges with the infinite cosmic potential that is not subject to impermanence or interdependence—that is unborn, uncreated, without beginning or end, the eternal reality of *ku.*

In *ku* there is nothing that pertains to the fields of sight, hearing, smell, touch, taste. As there is no environment, there is also nothing to observe and no subject to observe it—no consciousness. It is the total end. Absolute nothing.

If there are no more eyes, there is no more form, no more visual perception. And since one cannot see, nothing arises out of the faculty of seeing. If no relationship is established between the organ-subject and phenomenon-object, there is no *shiki* that can appear, and consciousness cannot manifest itself.

The original source of the mind is not ignorance or darkness. It is completely pure.

Before birth, humans are ignorance. Birth is the actualization of matter, the incarnation of their ignorant consciousness, which has been dwelling in the eternal consciousness during transmigration. Ignorance is the agent that produces action or karma. Transposed onto the human level, this primordial factor, ignorance, is divided in two: on one side, the ignorance of the parents leading to the karmic sexual act that brings about fecundation; on the other, the karmic ignorance in the consciousness of the being that has died and wants to be incarnated, which influences the parents' sexual act.

Those two interdependent causes lead to the formation of the embryo. The dead being's consciousness is incarnated at the instant of fecundation, itself a manifestation of cosmic energy. So the three elements that determine the appearance of the fetus— father, mother, and the consciousness of the dead being—are all equally responsible. Responsibility does not lie only with the parents, because past karma wants to be realized and has to find a physical medium in which to manifest itself.

Satori exists only in relation to ignorance and illusion; so ignorance and illusion are the necessary conditions for the existence of satori. And it is said, *bonno soku bodai*—illusions are not different from satori.

So it is not necessary to try to eliminate ignorance, because it has no more real existence than we ourselves.

An illusion is not something fixed, not the substance of our minds; it is a visitor, a thing that comes from outside. For example, anger, ignorance, fear, anxiety, passion, desires. No waves can appear on the surface of a lake unless there is wind. It is the same with illusions. If there is no external stimulus, they do not come. They are visitors from outside. Even if there is stimulus from the environment, though, we can deal wisely with them when they come, so long as we are not attached.

Suffering is physical as well as psychological, sentimental, intellectual, or rational. As soon as we cannot satisfy our desires, we suffer. Buddha explains suffering. The more attached we are, the more illusions develop that we cannot satisfy, so in the end we commit suicide. Being too attached to desires is being like a bomb.

The more our desires increase, the more complicated our sufferings become.

All the phenomena of the cosmos, all the existences of the cosmos, make up the temporary potential that exists or is manifest, actualized, in the instant. Each existence depends upon the law of interdependence, and the multiplicity of phenomena depends upon the multiplicity of relationships underlying them. So although these temporary phenomena take form when they are born, are transformed while they live, and then vanish, their substance has been neither produced nor destroyed, has increased no more than it has diminished. For that substance is the fundamental cosmic power itself, eternally immutable, the supreme potential from which proceed all phenomenal potentials, the endlessly changing existences whose forms appear at the behest of strictly ordered cosmic interferences, and then disappear and disintegrate, freeing the essence that returns to its origin.